Copyright © Chris Beetles Ltd 2023
8 & 10 Ryder Street, St James's
London SW1Y 6QB
020 7839 7551
gallery@chrisbeetles.com
www.chrisbeetles.com

ISBN 978-1-914906-11-4

Cataloguing in publication data is
available from the British Library

A Chris Beetles Ltd Publication

Edited by Chris Beetles,
Alexander Beetles, Fiona Nickerson
and Pascale Oakley

Design by Jeremy Brook

Photography by Alper Goldenberg

Reproduction by www.cast2create.com

Colour separation and printing by
Geoff Neal Litho Limited

Front cover:
SPY (SIR LESLIE WARD) (1851-1922)
Lord Farquhar [no 60]

Back cover:
SPY (Sir Leslie Ward) (1851-1922)
Self Portrait [no 1]

This page:
AJM (Arthur H Marks) (ACTIVE 1889)
Harry Marks [no 40]

1	Self Portrait	4500		54	Mr Clement King Shorter	4500
2	General Trochu	8500		55	Mr Samuel Whitbread	3500
3	Dr Jackson, The Bishop of London	3500		56	The Earl of Eglinton and Winton	2750
4	Mr Alexander D. R. W Baillie-Cochrane MP	6500		57	Sir Lewis McIver, Bart, MP	1750
5	Mr George Bentinck, MP	7500		58	Mr John Gilbert Talbot, MP, DCL	2750
6	Mr Charles Gilpin, MP	2750		59	Major Ferdinand Esterhazy	4250
7	Mr William Powell Frith, RA	7500		60	Lord Farquhar	4500
8	Mr Washington Hibbert	4500		61	The Hon. Sir Walter Francis Hely-Hutchinson,	2750
9	Lord Otho Augustus Fitzgerald, MP	3500		62	The Chevalier De Souza Correa	2750
10	Mr Samuel Laing MP	3500		63	M. Théophile Delcassé	3500
11	The Earl of Harrington	4500		64	Lord Justice Williams	3500
12	The Earl of Desart	2750		65	Sir William George Granville Venables	
13	Sir Henry Drummond-Wolff, KCMG, MP	4500			Vernon Harcourt, PC, MP, QC	2750
14	Sir William Augustus Fraser, of Morar, Bart, MP	500		66	Ignace Jan Paderewski	7500
15	Sir John Charles Dalrymple Hay, Bart, MP	3500		67	Mr Arthur Yates	2750
16	Prince Edward of Saxe-Weimar	3500		68	Mr Arthur De Rothschild	6500
17	H.M. Christian William Ferdinand			69	Mr George Wyndham, MP	4500
	Adolphus George, King of Greece	4500		70	Lord Raglan	4500
18	Colonel Charles Napier Sturt	3500		71	The Earl of Rosebery	8500
19	Lord Kensington, MP	3500		72	Mr Charles Santley	2750
20	Sir George Bowyer, Bart, MP	4500		73	John Gordon Swift MacNeill, KC, MP	2750
21	Viscount Castlereagh, MP	3500		74	The Reverend Henry Montagu Villiers, MA	1750
22	Lord Headley	3500		75	Jan Kubelik	6500
23	M. Victorien Sardou	4500		76	The Earl of Shrewsbury and Talbot	6500
24	Colonel Lewis Guy Phillips	4500		77	Sir Alexander Campbell Mackenzie	4500
25	The Earl of Winchilsea and Nottingham	4500		78	The Reverend Edgar Sheppard	1750
26	Sir John George Tollemache Sinclair, Bart, MP	3500		79	Sir Hiram Stevens Maxim	6500
27	General Lord Chelmsford, GCB	2750		80	Mr Egerton Castle	4500
28	The Duke of Norfolk	6500		81	Robert Henry Bullock-Marsham	3500
29	Sir John Bennett	2750		82	The Dean of Westminster	2750
30	Charles Spencer Bateman			83	Mr Albert Brassey	2750
	Hanbury Kincaid-Lennox	3500		84	Mr Henry J Wood	7500
31	The Earl of Seafield	3500		85	Allan Aynesworth	2750
32	Mr Richard Quain, MD, FRS	4500		86	Sir Thomas Shaughnessy	6500
33	M. Paul Lessar	3500		87	Col. Frank Shuttleworth	3500
34	Sir James Taylor Ingham, MA, Knight	2750		88	Anatole France	7500
35	Mr George Granville Leveson-Gower	1750		89	R E Belilios	3750
36	Mr Charles Beilby Stuart-Wortley, MP	950		90	Archer Baker	3500
37	Lord Egerton of Tatton	2750		91	C Herbert Workman	3250
38	Mr Frank Lockwood, QC MP	4500		92	Mr Justice Scrutton	3500
39	The Hon. Sir Edward Ebenezer Kay	750		93	H.R.H The Prince of Wales	8500
40	Harry Marks	4500		94	The Hon Thomas H A E Cochrane, DL, JP	2750
41	Mr Geo Egerton	3500		95	Lord Stanley of Alderley	3500
42	Sir William Christopher Leng	4500		96	Beast of Burden	4500
43	Mr Arthur Bower Forwood, MP	3500		97	Lord Randolph Churchill	6500
44	Mr Reuben David Sassoon	6500		98	An Elegant Gentleman	1750
45	Mr George Frederic Watts, RA	7500		99	Gentleman with Hands in his Pockets	2250
46	Mr Edward Linley Sambourne	6500		100	George Grossmith Jr	6500
47	Sir Charles Synge Christopher Bowen	5500		101	Sir Benjamin Leonard Cherry	2250
48	Mr Edward Lloyd	1750		102	Walter L Gladstone of Court Hey	1750
49	Colonel William Cornwallis West, MP	4250		103	Mr Arthur ...	3500
50	Mr Walter Herries Pollock	4500		104	The Reporter	1750
51	Mr Fred Crisp	2750		105	The Prince of Wales at the Moulin Rouge	7500
52	Mr William Allan, MP	3500		106	Henry Lucy at Boodles	3500
53	'At Cowes'. The R.Y.S	4500				

PORTRAITS OF
Vanity Fair

The Charles Sigety Collection

CHRIS BEETLES GALLERY

CONTENTS

Opposite:
Charles Sigety

Charles Sigety *Vanity Fair* Collection

Charles 'Charlie' Sigety (1922-2014) was a classic American success story. He was a visionary business and public service leader. He was an entrepreneur, healthcare pioneer, New York Real Estate developer, and a passionate collector of art and documents.

Born and raised by Hungarian immigrant parents in the Parkchester section of the Bronx, New York City, he graduated from Townsend Harris High School, Columbia University, Harvard Business School (HBS), and Yale Law School. His career combined entrepreneurial success with distinguished public service. During World War II, he served on a heavy cruiser, the USS *Fall River* as an Ensign in the Navy Supply Corps. After the war he graduated from Yale Law School, taught accounting at Pratt Institute and Yale, and became Assistant to the Commission on Federal Taxation at the American Institute of Accountants. In the 1950s, he served in the Eisenhower Administration as Deputy Commissioner of the Federal Housing Administration, and later returned to New York as a first Assistant Attorney General, and was also named the head of the NY State Housing Finance Agency.

An HBS course called 'The Management of New Enterprises,' or entrepreneurship, would profoundly influence his business life. In the early 1950's he co-founded Video Vittles Inc. with his wife, known professionally as Kit Kinne, who was the On Air Food Editor of NBC's early daytime TV show, *The Home Show*. He created Metropolitan Ski Slopes, bringing downhill skiing to NYC's Van Cortlandt Park in 1962, and founded the Florence Nightingale Health Center in Manhattan in 1965. In 1982, he and his family purchased Professional Medical Products Inc., a former medical device manufacturing subsidiary of Parke Davis Corporation headquartered in Greenwood, South Carolina. He was also an active real estate developer, primarily in New York City and Bucks County, Pennsylvania.

Mr. Sigety's philanthropic interests focused around educational institutions, giving both his time and resources to the Navy Supply School Foundation, Townsend Harris Alumni Association, Cazenovia College, Delaware Valley College, The Harvard Business School Alumni Association and the National Association for Continence. He was also an active member of the Confrérie des Chevaliers du Tastevin, and Confrérie de la Chaîne des Rôtisseurs where he honed his love of fine food and wine.

Charlie Sigety was an avid and passionate collector of wine, historic memorabilia, particularly documents, and art. Over many years, Mr Sigety enthusiastically collected in a remarkably wide range of fields. Art was a central theme from the beginning. Among the many drawings, watercolours and paintings, he collected important works of American illustration by Maxfield Parrish, J C Leyendecker, Norman Rockwell, and others. His Americana collection also featured original comic drawings and caricatures, by Al Hirschfeld, Ernie Bushmiller, Morris Weiss and others; rare books and first editions including the seminal *Federalist Papers* (1788), urging ratification of the Constitution; a Peter Force printing of *The Declaration of Independence*; a fine multi-volume set of the *Journals of Congress* and a book from George Washington's library (*The Adventures of Gil Blas*, 1775).

Mr. Sigety found original letters and documents fascinating, and amassed a sizeable quantity of presidential and historical documents, featuring at least six signed by Thomas Jefferson as well as items signed or written by George Washington, Abraham Lincoln, William Henry Harrison, Sam Houston, Patrick Henry ('give me liberty or give me death'), Ben Franklin and other American patriots. His New York roots were reflected in important documents from the earliest days of New Amsterdam, such as two Peter Stuyvesant documents.

His interests in books and manuscripts were cosmopolitan, stretching beyond the United States. He possessed a 1482 Ptolemy map of the world and a strong series of illustrated ornithological folios with spectacular hand coloured illustrations after Marc Catesby, John Gould, Pierre Levaillant and others.

The Charles E. Sigety *Vanity Fair* Collection is a tribute to Charlie's passion for collecting British illustration art, and his collection of original *Vanity Fair* caricatures is extensive. This exhibition is thereby giving other collectors the chance to enjoy the fruits gathered by this passionate and remarkable man.

Sigety Family
2023

Charles Sigety (1922-2014) –
Chris Beetles Remembers

During 50 years as an art dealer, I have met many famous and high achieving men, a modern panoply of *Vanity Fair*; energetic and ambitious politicians, vibrant and obsessive sportsmen, inspired musicians and composers, soldiers of mixed fortune, figurative artists washed in tradition, fiction writers, chroniclers of our times, self-assured landed gentry, judges and barristers, stimulating polemicists all.

I have spent a life of preferment with privileged contacts and so they line the pages of my memory just like the pages of the Victorian publication *Vanity Fair*, which displayed the high and mighty of the age, slightly caricatured, moderately satirical, always celebratory and all in full length with an apposite costume, striking images of certainty for a self-confident age. But none, past or present, linger more happily in my memory than Charles Sigety, one of the most remarkable men I have ever met.

Charles Sigety is of course the classic case of the second-generation American success story from the European Diaspora. His achievements, his philanthropy, and wide intellectual and entrepreneurial reach is listed well on the previous page. He wore it all lightly, always moving on at pace to new sights, new sensations and new friendships.

In February 1996, I was the latest recipient to be plugged into the electrical grid that was Charles Sigety. He visited the gallery (lost trying to find his way to Christie's front door), introduced himself and immediately interrogated me on my stock. Charles took up a lot of space, most of it his personality. He was built like an all-in wrestler with a warm self-confident engagement and a smile that hid nothing.

'I don't suppose you have any *Vanity Fair* originals?'
'Yes, we have one of the famous Victorian painter, G F Watts.'
'Good, I'll take it. Have you heard of Al Hirschfeld?'
'Of course, we have one of Neville Marriner, the famous conductor.'
'Good, I'll take it.'

That exchange, full of trust and mutual regard was the start of a shared enthusiasm that never faltered until his death 20 years later that cut short his life-time ambition. Charles Sigety wanted to publish a book and stage a major show of his collection of *Vanity Fair* original artworks. In particular he wanted to recreate the great reputation of Sir Leslie Ward (Spy) whose recording of an age of personal achievement and advances in society he approved. His loving family and inheritors understand that and desire to carry out the wishes of their beloved patriarch.

Whenever I visited New York he would scoop me up and take me to his own restaurant, 'Café des Artistes', where we would rejoice in the exuberant murals of Howard Chandler Christy, and of course eat copiously. Charles' appetite was voracious and only matched by his omnivorous curiosity for life in the Big Apple. His conversational style was didactic, so much of this would be retold to me as he drove me about his beloved New York where I learned much about 'Air Rights', immigrant demographics, Public Health, and the 'Jarndycian' foolishness of the laws delays.

On one of these guided tours shortly after 9/11, he took me downtown to see the ghastly aftermath. I do not know how he managed to get himself into the heavily guarded site but he drove his 4x4 into and around the moonscape that was now Ground Zero. Here, he expanded on the wrongs of history and religion but said that he felt optimistic for the next generation and a building of a better world, based on shared values between our two countries. To hear these words in such an area of desolation made me realise that I was listening to a very special, wise and compassionate man.

So, Sir Leslie Ward, where is your sketch pad? You have another name to add to the roll call of the Charles Sigety Collection of *Vanity Fair*. He is Charles Sigety himself, an unforgettable man who leaves you his unforgettable collection.

Dr Chris Beetles
2023

Vanity Fair

'I venture to prophesy that, when the history of the Victorian Era comes to be written in true perspective, the most faithful mirror and record of representative men and the spirit of their times will be sought and found in Vanity Fair'

(Leslie Ward, *Forty Years of 'Spy',* page 331)

When, on 7 November 1868, the first edition of the new 'society journal' *Vanity Fair* was published, there was little indication within its pages of the influence it was to have on Victorian high society. This first edition contained no caricatures, its text commented on the week's social and political events and reviewed the latest literary and theatrical releases. The journal failed to find immediate success and struggled to compete with other more established papers such as *The Owl* and *The Tomahawk. Vanity Fair*'s founder, Thomas Gibson Bowles, was the son of a prominent liberal politician, Thomas Milner Gibson, and his wife, Susannah Arethusa Gibson, who was well established in influential social circles and regularly hosted fashionable salons. Growing up within this environment, Bowles was able to socialise with journalists, actors, artists, politicians and bohemians. Whilst maintaining a junior position at the Board of Trade, he began to contribute to various journals, including *The Glow Worm, The Owl* and *The Tomahawk.* Though it was his experiences with these publications that gave Bowles the confidence to create his own journal, it was his social connections that not only helped it get off the ground, but also shaped its future. A close friend, Colonel Frederick Gustavus Burnaby, supplied £100 of the £200 original investment and, although Bowles wrote much of the text himself under the pseudonym 'Jehu Junior', he engaged regular contributors to participate. These contributors were selected from fashionable sets for their social as much as their literary qualifications. Indeed, *Vanity Fair* was written by and for the Victorian and Edwardian establishment.

On 16 January 1869, Bowles promised his readers 'Some Pictorial Wares of an entirely novel character'. What was to follow not only set *Vanity Fair* apart from its competitors, but changed the way in which caricature was viewed and received. Two weeks later, a full-page caricature of Benjamin Disraeli by Carlo Pellegrini appeared in *Vanity Fair*, followed the next week by a caricature of William Gladstone. The images were reproduced by the highly regarded lithographer, Vincent Brooks, using an approach that was virtually unprecedented in England. Until this point, lithography had been reserved largely for topographical and decorative subjects. Cartoons and caricatures, such as those published in popular satirical magazines like *Punch*, were reproduced through wood-engraving. Pellegrini's caricatures, completed under the pseudonym 'Singe', were the first of over 2,300 caricatures to be published in *Vanity Fair.* These highly-skilled, lithographically reproduced, full-page cartoons, in a journal published in quarto dimensions with eight to ten pages per issue, gave *Vanity Fair* an instant identity.

Carlo Pellegrini collaborated with Thomas Gibson Bowles and Vincent Brooks with enormous success. A favourite of the Prince of Wales, the immensely popular Neapolitan mixed easily with his subjects and portrayed them gently, making it something of a mark of honour, even a social necessity, to appear in *Vanity Fair*'s pages.

Leslie Ward, 1921

Before then, the nature of English caricature had been shaped by the savage work of the Georgian cartoonists such as Thomas Rowlandson and James Gillray. Pellegrini diluted the ferocity of these cartoons through his own style, influenced by his early years caricaturing bohemian society in Naples, and by the work of his fellow Neapolitan, Melchiorre Delfico (who would later contribute eight drawings to *Vanity Fair*). The gently humorous style of caricature that was introduced to England by the likes of Pellegrini and Delfico was immediately more palatable to the sensibilities of Victorian Society than the more brutal satire made popular in France.

The success of Carlo Pellegrini and the burgeoning popularity of *Vanity Fair* made the magazine an attractive proposition for foreign artists seeking patronage in the upper echelons of society. In 1869 the French society painter, James Tissot, began to contribute under the pseudonym 'Coïdé', bringing a more serious, portraiture style to the magazine. This suited the preferences of Thomas Bowles Gibson, but understanding that Pellegrini's more satirical drawings were what had brought him success, sought other more humorous collaborators to work alongside him. These included Adriano Cecioni, Melchiorre Delfico, Francis Carruthers Gould and the American political cartoonist, Thomas Nast.

The arrival of Leslie Ward at *Vanity Fair* in 1873 turned the magazine into a national institution. Drawing under the pseudonym 'Spy', Ward was industrious, dependable and passionate. Bowles Gibson came to rely on him over the mercurial Pellegrini, who left *Vanity Fair* on a number of occasions to pursue other ventures. For 40 years, 'Spy' caricatured the highest profile figures in Victorian society, from actors and sportsmen to politicians and royalty. Having grown up rubbing shoulders with those whom he now caricatured, through his family connections and personal acquaintances, he was able to move easily in these social circles. He considered himself no bohemian, rather he saw himself as a professional, dedicated to his craft. To be caricatured by 'Spy' and for the result to appear in *Vanity Fair* was a confirmation of one's importance to Victorian society.

Though Leslie Ward's approach to his art changed the perception of caricature in Victorian England, it was not always for the better. In *Vanity Fair*'s early days, this respectable, often flattering form of caricature was something entirely new. In the light of this novelty, it was viewed in the right spirit by those portrayed. Later, as Ward lamented in his autobiography, *Forty Years of Spy*, those he drew began to grow particular and demanding about how they were represented. Ward began his career at *Vanity Fair* physically seeking out his subjects around London; as he grew busier, he began to request that many came to sit for him at his studio. Frequently, he received sitters who would pay for the privilege of being caricatured. This opened an entirely new form of subject to him, and with it came a more commercial relationship between Ward and his sitters.

Despite the ongoing success of *Vanity Fair*, the attentions of Thomas Gibson Bowles had begun to focus elsewhere by the 1880s, and he was content to leave most of the illustrations to Leslie Ward. He had become more involved in politics (he would become Conservative MP for King's Lynn in 1892) and had other newspaper interests including *The Lady*, which he founded in 1884. In 1889, he sold *Vanity Fair* for £20,000 and was replaced as editor by A G Witherby. Although this did not immediately alter the character of the magazine, the death of Pellegrini in January 1889 left Ward as the only experienced member of staff. For the next decade, the only other regular contributor of illustrations was the French caricaturist, Jean Baptiste Guth.

Though some have argued that *Vanity Fair* fell into a decline in the twentieth century, having lost some of its wit and irreverence, it remained a proving ground for aspiring young artists, the most notable being Max Beerbohm, who contributed nine drawings to the magazine in its later years. *Vanity Fair*'s final caricature, of Joseph Chamberlain drawn by 'Astz', was published on 14 January 1914. The following month, it was absorbed by *Hearth and Home*.

Other periodicals founded during this period purported to be society papers, but none came close to matching *Vanity Fair*. This was undoubtedly due to the consistent quality of cartoons from the likes of Ward and Pellegrini. Ward described *Mayfair*, a paper he occasionally drew for, as 'the only Society journal that I can recall having succeeded in any way on the lines of *Vanity Fair*' [*Forty Years of 'Spy'*, page 337]. A comment published in *The Week*, a Canadian journal, on 3 April 1884, claimed that whilst it was virtually unknown outside of London, *Vanity Fair* 'owes the small place it holds in flunkeydom to the clever cartoons of public characters which appear each week'.

Though *Vanity Fair* was, like many other similar magazines, a purveyor of 'backstairs court and aristocratic tittle-tattle' (as described by *The Week)*, Leslie Ward described *Vanity Fair* in his autobiography as the first magazine that could rightfully call itself a society journal. Through the acerbic wit of Thomas Gibson Bowles and other contributors, and through the caricatures of 'Spy', *Vanity Fair* became the essential representation of Victorian high society, a paper written by and for the Establishment.

Further Reading:
Roy T. Matthews, Peter Mellini, *In 'Vanity Fair'*, Berkeley, CA: University of California Press, 1982
Leslie Ward, *Forty Years of 'Spy'*, London: Chatto & Windus, 1915

1
Spy (Sir Leslie Ward) (1851-1922)
Self Portrait
Signed and inscribed 'Leslie Ward'
Watercolour and bodycolour with pencil
13 x 7 ½ inches

COÏDÉ (JAMES TISSOT) (1836-1902)
General Trochu

Louis-Jules Trochu (1815-1896) had served with distinction in the French armed forces during the Crimean War. During the Franco-Prussian War, he was appointed Governor of Paris and commander-in-chief of all forces responsible for the defence of the capital. The leadership he demonstrated during the Siege of Paris saw him named President of the Government of National Defence, the de facto head of state, on 4 September 1870.

'The Hope of France'

"General Trochu, whose very name was, except to military men, a fortnight ago, utterly unknown, has suddenly been placed in, perhaps, the most difficult position in Europe, and the eyes of the whole civilised world are bent upon him to see how he will acquit himself of the responsibility he has assumed. When the system that has ruled France for the last eighteen years collapsed, when, with her soil invaded, her last army destroyed, the Empire crumbled ignominiously into dust, and the hated Prussian marching on Paris, France arose, bleeding but beautiful, among the ruins, the cry went forth for a man to save the country in its peril. It is the greatest possible testimony that could be afforded of the belief in the ability of General Trochu that at this supreme moment all men and all parties turned to him as to the most patriotic and trustworthy, and that they should have acclaimed him chief of the little band on whom France relies to save her from present destruction.

As President of the Provisional Government, General Trochu has achieved miracles of energy. He cares little for the vain trappings of war, but there is no one who is so well acquainted with the use of its various weapons. His name has long been known as that of an able theorist upon military organisation; he has now established his fame as a practical worker-out of his theories. In four days he gathered up an army from the remotest corners of France and placed them in Paris, drilled, armed, equipped, and ready for the fray. The defence of Paris and of France, however, although the first, is not the greatest, part of his task. When the last Prussian shall have quitted the country his difficulties will only have begun, and it remains to be seen how he will be able to deal first with the Orleanists and next with the Socialists, who will work in different directions to make the Republic impossible. He is himself accused of being a friend of the D'Orléans, but he is known to be first of all a patriot, and he will assuredly seek only with a single mind to interpret and to carry out the will of his country. He is the hope of France, and should he succeed in freeing her from the foreign enemy, he will become the President of a Republic in which his mission will be to preserve her from internal foes."

Vanity Fair, 17 September 1870

2
COÏDÉ (JAMES TISSOT) (1836-1902)
General Trochu
'The Hope of France'
Ink and watercolour with pencil and chalk
11 ¾ x 7 inches
Illustrated: *Vanity Fair*, 17 September 1870, Men of the Day no 10,
'The Hope of France'

APE (CARLO PELLEGRINI) (1839-1889)
Dr Jackson, The Bishop of London

In 1868, John Jackson (1811-1885) was named Bishop of London by Benjamin Disraeli, replacing Archibald Tait, following his translation to Archbishop of Canterbury. Jackson had been rector of St James's, Piccadilly in 1846, a chaplain to Queen Victoria in 1847, an honorary canon of Bristol Cathedral in 1852 and, from 1853, Bishop of Lincoln. He served as Bishop of London until his death in 1885.

'One Who Has Grieved More Than Others Over "The Sinfulness of Little Sins"'

"The Bishop of London is a prelate against whom no unkind word was ever spoken, as, on the other hand, he is a remarkable example of the large measure of worldly success which is often attained by unworldly men. He is an Oxford scholar, and has been a Boyle lecturer. On the summit of Muswell Hill, two or three bowshots from the residence of Mr. Mudie, the great librarian, there stands an ivy-covered church, with a slender spire, pointing the way that Mr. Mudie should in duty go, and, let us hope, is going – not too fast, for we cannot very well spare him – heavenwards. Of this church Dr. Jackson was appointed curate when it was erected, some thirty years ago, at the instance of Canon Harvey, the Rector of Hornsey. He then became master of the Islington Grammar School; and when the late Bishop Bloomfield offered the living of St. James's, Westminster, to Mr. Harvey, the latter feeling a preference for his rural retreat, and perfectly satisfied of the harmlessness, combined with a respectable amount of earnestness, and any amount of sincerity and hard work, of his friend Jackson, recommended him for the preferment, and his recommendation was adopted. From St. James's, Dr. Jackson was translated direct – without going through the purgatorial experiences of a Deanery – to the heaven of Episcopacy, as Bishop of Lincoln, the good city over which the devil in former times used to look with envy, on account of its numerous steeples. In 1869, when Bishop Tait went to Canterbury, people were surprised to see the good Bishop of Lincoln removed to the See of London. So far, however, the experiment has been a successful one, as the lion of Tractarianism has since lain quietly down with the lamb of Evangelicalism, and something as nearly as possible approaching to a little child in spirit leads them. The works of Dr. Jackson are highly creditable to the Episcopal functions. He has ten or twelve daughters. He has grieved more than others over 'The Sinfulness of Little Sins.' His 'Christian Character' is highly esteemed; and his 'Repentance' has been much talked of. As Dr. Jackson has had the good sense and the necessary tact to keep out of hot water in the See of London, there is a reasonable ground for hope that he will be as successful hereafter, as he has been hitherto, in avoiding the snares of Satan."

Vanity Fair, 12 November 1870

3
APE (CARLO PELLEGRINI) (1839-1889)
Dr Jackson, The Bishop of London
'One Who Has Grieved More Than Others Over "The Sinfulness of Little Sins"'
Signed
Watercolour with bodycolour
12 x 7 ½ inches
Provenance: Thomas Gibson Bowles; The John Franks Collection
Illustrated: *Vanity Fair*, 12 November 1870, Statesmen no 69,
'One Who Has Grieved More Than Others Over "The Sinfulness of Little Sins"'

CoÏdÉ (James Tissot) (1836-1902)
Mr Alexander D R W Baillie-Cochrane MP

By early 1841 Alexander Baillie-Cochrane (1816-1890) was a leading member, with Lord John Manners and G S Smythe, of what Disraeli by then was calling 'Young England'. In that summer's general election, he stood unsuccessfully at Bridport as a Conservative, but was elected in September as a Liberal-Conservative. Between 1864 and 1868, he was joint editor and writer for *The Owl*, a popular satirical weekly. At the time of his caricature in *Vanity Fair*, he was MP for the Isle of Wight.

'Judicious Amelioration'

"Although of Scotch extraction, and a descendant of Sir William Wallace, Mr Baillie-Cochrane sits in the House of Commons as a Conservative; but being always anxious to adopt and to follow a line of his own, he is generally found professing a Conservatism removed from the kind that does every-day duty. Taking a part in most of the important debates, he may generally be reckoned upon to approach his subject from a point of view differing more or less from those hitherto occupied. An advocate of 'judicious amelioration' rather than of obstinate conservation, it is but a few months since that he angered his political friends by frankly announcing himself as a convert to the Ballot before they were quite ready to take the same step; and that he shocked his party by adducing among his reasons a belief in the 'Conservative tendencies' of the working-classes, and a desire to rescue them from the tyranny of clubs and committees. He takes, moreover, an especial interest in, and has some special acquaintance with, the foreign politics with which so few concern themselves; and he is the one Member of the House of Commons who has shown that he is aware of the treachery involved in the successful efforts made by England to rob France of her intended allies in the late war. Not being open to the imputation of aspiring to office, his opinions are always taken for what they are worth. He is alive to the charms of the fair sex; he has a presence and a delivery which never fail to win for him sympathy in his oratorical efforts; and being at no loss for extracts of prose or verse wherewith to ornament his speeches, he is suspected of cultivating society and polite literature, and of a design to say things new and true in a way that shall at once please and convince."

Vanity Fair, 12 February 1871

4
CoÏdÉ (James Tissot) (1836-1902)
Mr Alexander D R W Baillie-Cochrane MP
'Judicious Amelioration'
Inscribed 'B Cochrane' and dated '12 Decr 71' on reverse
Watercolour on tinted paper
12 x 7 ½ inches
Illustrated: *Vanity Fair*, 12 February 1871, Statesmen no 98, 'Judicious Amelioration'

VANITY FAIR.   Aug. 5th, 1871.

No. 144.   STATESMEN, No. 90.
"Big Ben."

COÏDÉ (JAMES TISSOT) (1836-1902)
Mr George Bentinck, MP

George Bentinck (1803-1886) was the Conservative MP for Norfolk West in the periods 1852-65 and 1871-84. Known for being bluff, outspoken and highly independent, he was nicknamed 'Big Ben'.

On 23 December 1871, *Vanity Fair* published Tissot's caricature of George Cavendish-Bentinck (1821-1891), who was then Conservative MP for Whitehaven. A cousin of 'Big Ben', he was known in Parliamentary circles as 'Little Ben'.

'Big Ben'

"We are occasionally reminded that there are still left in the House of Commons a few men to represent that sincere and deep-seated Toryism which is embodied in a set of principles honestly believed by their professors to be wholesome, and forming a creed which neither time nor circumstances can modify. Mr. Bentinck – or, as he is affectionately called even by his strongest opponents, 'Big Ben' – is the most thorough-going exponent of that belief now in public life. His political principles are so obsolete in the present day that no party can be found ready to give effect to them, nor any chiefs willing to profess and to stand by them; but Mr. Bentinck has a sincerity of conviction in them which nothing can shake, and deserted as they have been by all, he still stands fast, and regards with undisguised scorn the men who have bartered the ancient beliefs for place and power. He never loses an occasion to attack the Liberal chiefs who are, as he believes, bringing the country to ruin, and he is as constant and even more unsparing in his denunciation of the Conservatives who have proved false to the faith he holds. The two front benches have so many weak places that he is at no loss to find daily matter for his fierce attacks. His language is plain and bold to an extent which often brings him into conflict with the rules of debate, but his reproaches are too well-founded in truth to be easily disposed of, and the leaders on both sides, although they writhe under his lash, have come to the conclusion that the only course to take is that of silent and unanswering endurance of the punishment.

'Big Ben' has all those generous qualities and manly tastes which we delight to attribute specially to the Englishman. He is an ardent lover of field sports, and of all the more vigorous pastimes that are pursued in this country. He delights above all things in the sea, and, holding, probably, that houses were only invented in order to keep ships' stores in, prefers to live upon it as the natural element of man. A proficient himself in practical knowledge of seamanship, and of all that appertains to navigation, he regards the ordinary fair-weather yachtsman with a pitying contempt nearly equal to that which he entertains for fair-weather politicians. He is withal, what with his qualities he could not fail to be, one of the most popular of men, and certainly the most popular of any who hold opinions so opposed as his are to the spirit and tendencies of the times."

Vanity Fair, 5 August 1871

5
COÏDÉ (JAMES TISSOT) (1836-1902)
Mr George Bentinck, MP
'Big Ben'
Watercolour, pencil and charcoal
12 x 7 ½ inches
Illustrated: *Vanity Fair*, 5 August 1871, Statesmen no 90, 'Big Ben'
Literature: Michael Justin Wentworth, *James Tissot: Catalogue Raisonné of His Prints*, Minneapolis, MN: Institute of Arts, Sterling and Francine Clark Art Institute, 1978, page 348

VANITY FAIR.   Jan. 18, 1873.

No. 111.   STATESMEN No. 136.
"Capital Punishment."

MELCHIORRE DELFICO (1825-1895)
Mr Charles Gilpin, MP

Moving to London from his hometown of Bristol in 1842, Charles Gilpin (1815-1874) began work as a publisher, publishing a large number of memoirs of the lives of Quakers and also launched and published *The Friend*, an evangelical Quaker magazine. Though he was defeated at a by-election for Perth in 1852, he successfully stood as Liberal MP for Northampton in 1857, 1859, 1865 and 1874. Between 1859 and 1865, he served as Secretary of the Poor Law Board under Lord Palmerston, a surprising appointment considering that Gilpin's opposition to the Conspiracy to Murder Bill of 1858 played a role in the Prime Minister's resignation in 1859.

'Capital Punishment'

"A man who is born with the beliefs of his time, and a moderate amount of energy is certain if he can steer clear of scrapes and death to make for himself a decent position. And Mr. Gilpin is such a man. He came into the world now sixty-eight years ago, of a middle-class Quaker family in the middle-class City of Bristol, and has pursued that even career of prosperity which a simple attachment to current platitudinarian reforms often insures. He started as a publisher in Manchester, but removed his business to London, where he soon made himself sufficiently remarked to obtain a seat in the City Common Council. Being ready of speech he was held among the Councilmen for an orator and a statesman, which enabled him to pass an address to Kossuth, to procure the abolition of street-tolls, and to look forward to such a larger sphere of action as might become the nephew of Joseph Sturge and the friend of Cobden.

Mr. Gilpin's first appearance in public life had been as a Sunday-school teacher, and he has throughout his career retained much of the Sunday-school cast of thought. He has identified himself with all the social palliatives that modern ingenuity has invented, and belongs to untold societies of the benevolent intention kind. He is great in the Anti-Slavery Movement; he is for Universal Peace for Ragged Schools, for Financial Reform for Temperance, for Idiot Asylums for Free Trade, for Orphanages for Everybody, and above all for the Abolition of Capital Punishment, which he holds to be a dangerously uncertain kind of penalty to inflict upon a man. He is for commerce naturally and has hitherto been known as a pillar of the speculations with which he has had to do. In Parliament he has sat for Northampton during the last sixteen years, and he is occasionally listened to with interest by a considerable number of members – so much so that in 1859 Lord Palmerston made him Secretary to the Poor Law Board, a post which he resigned in 1864. He has not since been requested to accept office, but has contented himself with forwarding petitions for condemned convicts and expounding the views of the more active of the well-meaners."

Vanity Fair, 18 January 1873

6
MELCHIORRE DELFICO (1825-1895)
Mr Charles Gilpin, MP
'Capital Punishment'
Signed
Watercolour and pencil with bodycolour on tinted paper
12 x 7 ¼ inches
Provenance: Thomas Gibson Bowles;
The John Franks Collection
Illustrated: *Vanity Fair*, 18 January 1873, Statesmen no 136,
'Capital Punishment'

SPY (SIR LESLIE WARD) (1851-1922)
Mr William Powell Frith, RA

William Powell Frith (1819-1909) was a leading Victorian genre painter and Royal Academician, considered to be one of the greatest British painters of social scenes. Works such as *The Railway Station* (1862), *Ramsgate Sands* (1854) and what is considered his masterwork, *The Derby Day* (1856-58), were met with almost universal acclaim when they were presented at the Royal Academy of Arts.

'The Derby-Day'

"The glories of the English school of painting have faded sadly since the days of Reynolds, and even since those of Turner; nor is there perhaps any save Millais to whom we can point as a contemporary national master. Mr. Frith nevertheless has won much popularity, for which indeed he has worked in a steady, sober, industrious manner, and with considerable intelligence. He was born in Yorkshire fifty-four years ago, and unlike so many great men who have been driven out of other into artistic pursuits by the sheer force of their love for them, was apprenticed to art at the early age of sixteen. He observed the taste of the day, and painted for it genre pictures from Shakespeare, Sterne, and Dickens, attempting occasionally the historical or the medieval variety of subject. His pictures have always met with the success that must attend the presentation, not perhaps of the highest, or best, or truest, but of the most popular view of a given thing or situation. His manipulation and colouring too are quite according to the current taste of the masses, so that when he tells a tale with his brush most of those who witness the result feel that he has told it precisely as they would have conceived and told it themselves. His most famous picture, 'The Derby Day', is an instance of this, and is in fact a reproduction of the articles that may be met any year in any of the daily newspapers. Mr. Frith does not take us far, but he takes us by the ways we understand, wherefore many of us think him a great painter. He does not enter deeply into life, but he can paint its incidents as they appear from the outside, and he has laboured consistently to show as much of the outside as is possible to a generation which often cannot perceive even that.

In himself Mr. Frith is an amiable pleasant man of the ordinary English type, and exceedingly like his pictures. It is no small thing to say of him that he is entirely free from artistic jealousy, and that he has more than once extended to young artists that helping hand which has enabled them to achieve a position and success."

Vanity Fair, 10 May 1873

7
SPY (SIR LESLIE WARD) (1851-1922)
Mr William Powell Frith, RA
'The Derby-Day'
Signed
Watercolour with bodycolour on tinted paper
12 x 7 ¼ inches
Provenance: The Forbes Collection
Illustrated: *Vanity Fair*, 10 May 1873, Men of the Day no 63, **'The Derby-Day'**

VANITY FAIR.   June 28, 1873.

No. 143.   MEN OF THE DAY, No. 65.
'A Londoner'

COÏDÉ (JAMES TISSOT) (1836-1902)
Mr Washington Hibbert

John Hubert Washington Hibbert (1804-1875) was born into a family made wealthy by a slave factorage business in Kingston. His father died when Washington Hibbert was young, leaving him a large inheritance. With this money he embarked upon a number of ambitious architectural projects, in partnership with the architect Augustus Pugin, best known for designing the interior of the Palace of Westminster.

'A Londoner'

"The old type of English gentleman – with a special individuality of his own, with a high sense of honour, and a thorough belief in the obligation that lies upon a man of family to act up to the traditions of his race – has so nearly disappeared in the crowd of glorified shopkeepers fitted with dress and principles made each like unto the other by wholesale, that it is pleasant and refreshing to find, as is found in Mr. Washington Hibbert, one who neither is nor strives to appear as though he were merely of the crowd. His outward appearance is well-known in London, and it impresses at once as that of a man of a special character and a special distinction, made all the more evident through being translated in other modes than those current among the ordinary. In fact, Mr. Washington Hibbert is one of those whose position and standing enable them to be a law to themselves in external matters precisely because in matters more important they follow the law in which they believe. Of an ancient family, and holding still to the original faith that England professed when the greatest of the great deeds were done that have made her what she is, he has led for now seventy years a tranquil, honourable, and honoured life; and although a country gentleman is so confirmed a Londoner that he never sleeps out of the metropolis. His houses have long been known for a grateful yet unpretending hospitality, presided over by a lady who while one of the most popular hostesses in London, has shown upon occasion that she too believes in higher principles than those of Commerce, and that she too holds that an English gentleman's house and family should not be dealt with on Chapman's principles."

Vanity Fair, 28 June 1873

8
COÏDÉ (JAMES TISSOT) (1836-1902)
Mr Washington Hibbert
'A Londoner'
Watercolour with bodycolour and pencil
12 ¼ x 7 ½ inches
Provenance: Thomas Gibson Bowles;
The John Franks Collection
Illustrated: *Vanity Fair*, 28 June 1873, Men of the Day no 65,
'A Londoner'

SPY (SIR LESLIE WARD) (1851-1922)
The Right Honourable Lord Otho Augustus Fitzgerald, MP

Lord Otho Augustus Fitzgerald (1827-1882) began his career in the army, serving as an officer in the Royal Horse Guards and as a Gentleman of the Bedchamber to the Lord-Lieutenant of Ireland. His political career began in 1865 as Liberal MP for Kildare, a seat that he held until 1874. In 1866, he was sworn of the Privy Council and made Treasurer of the Household under Lord Russell. In 1868, he was appointed Comptroller of the Household under William Gladstone, which he held until 1874. He was also known as a talented amateur composer, publishing several piano compositions in Dublin.

'A Message From The Queen'

"To be well-born, good looking, amiable to all comers, and ready of speech on most occasions is, as times go in England, to have all the chances. Even with these chances, however, it is perhaps not possible for any to be at once popular with men and a favourite with women, for the qualities and conduct required for success in one of these two respects are precisely those which often bring about failure in the other. Men as a rule endure best the modesty which overlies the greater gifts or acquirements, women rather prefer that assurance which makes the most of the lesser. Yet Lord Otho Fitzgerald has among the men as many allies as he would wish for, while among the more discriminating sex he has moved all his life rather as a conqueror among tributaries than as one great Power treating with another. Born somewhat over forty years ago, he passed nine years in the affectionate fraternity of the Blues, who still retain the memory of his military career. He then became Master of the Horse to the Lord-Lieutenant of Ireland, and subsequently was made Gentleman of the Bedchamber and Treasurer of Her Majesty's Household, until at last he aimed at the dignity of Comptroller, in which capacity he appears from time to time in the House of Commons as the bearer of a message from the Queen. He sits there also as the elected of Kildare county, as which he is a Liberal, and therefore in favour of every change that has been tried to reconcile the Irish to the English occupation. He takes however but a comparatively small share in popular legislation or debate, and it is in the sacred circles of Society that he is best known. He is reputed at Cowes as a professor of seamanship, and he has gone through a serious course of successive steam-launches. On the whole a fortunate man, well-considered at Court, well-known in the world of fashion, and taking life and people with the good-temper that should always arise from success."

Vanity Fair, 9 August 1873

9
SPY (SIR LESLIE WARD) (1851-1922)
The Right Honourable Lord Otho
Augustus Fitzgerald, MP
'A Message From The Queen'
Signed
Watercolour and bodycolour with pencil
12 x 7 inches
Provenance: Thomas Gibson Bowles; Stanley Jackson;
The John Franks Collection
Illustrated: *Vanity Fair*, 9 August 1873, Statesmen no 150,
'A Message From The Queen'

VANITY FAIR.   Aug. 16, 1873.

No. 250.   STATESMEN, No. 151.
"The infant Samuel."

Spy (Sir Leslie Ward) (1851-1922)
Mr Samuel Laing, MP

Born in Edinburgh, Samuel Laing (1812-1897) was educated at St John's College, Cambridge, graduating in 1831 and was elected a fellow of St John's in 1834, remaining there for a period as a mathematical coach. He was called to the bar at Lincoln's Inn in November 1832 before being appointed Private Secretary to Henry Labouchere (afterward Lord Taunton), then President of the Board of Trade.

He was appointed secretary of the newly formed railway department in 1842 and was a significant contributor to Gladstone's Railway Act of 1844. In 1848 he was appointed Chairman and Managing Director of the London, Brighton, and South Coast Railway. He resigned in 1852 and entered politics, becoming Liberal MP for Wick and later, at the time of his appearance in *Vanity Fair*, MP for Orkney and Shetland. In 1860, he also served briefly as Financial Secretary to the Treasury before becoming Financial Minister to the Crown in India, a post he held until 1865. In 1866, he returned to his previous role at the London, Brighton, and South Coast Railway (who had struggled financially in his absence), remaining in the position until his retirement in 1894.

At the age of seventy and following his retirement from Parliament in 1885, Samuel Laing found further success in a new career as an author of accessible scientific and anthropological thought. His *Modern Science and Modern Thought* (1885) was widely read and was followed by *A Modern Zoroastrian* (1887), *Problems of the Future, and other Essays* (1889), *The Antiquity of Man* (1891) and *Human Origins* (1892).

'The infant Samuel'

"*A shrewd, practical, hard-headed man is Mr. Laing; a man of powerful intelligence, not to be misled by sophistry or by cheats conscious or unconscious: undoubtedly one of the superior order, naturally claiming and inevitably obtaining the leadership of men. Quite a personage is he, yet a disappointing personage withal; for being certain to succeed in any career he might choose, he has deliberately chosen the career of money-making, as being on the whole that which is, in these latter days, best worth an able man's attention. So that now, at the age of sixty, he is regarded as a second-rate statesmen because a first-rate financier, and as one whose life has proved a greater success for himself than for his generation; wherein there are perhaps more to assert that he is wrong than to act as though they believed it. Indeed it is no mean thing to have been concerned as Mr. Laing has been, and still is, in the superior direction of some of the most important commercial enterprises in the world; and possibly if all values were weighed in the same balance it would be found that the industrial work done in England under his guidance is more fruitful of results than the political evolutions through which many, vastly his inferiors, have won positions in the State superior to his. He is the king among the financiers. Whenever an enterprise of any magnitude is in more than ordinary difficulties the aid of 'the infant Samuel' is certain to be invoked – his mere opinion of a speculation is a guaranty of success; and although he has himself invested much money in venturesome ways, he has seen his wealth increase until he has become what he now is – one of the wealthy men of the country.*

He started in life with many advantages. He was a Scotchman. He was Second Wrangler at Cambridge. He was a barrister. He was private secretary to Mr. Labouchere, and subsequently the first Secretary of that Railway Department of the Board of Trade to the organisation of which he so strongly contributed. To railways indeed, as to the new great Power then about to be developed in the world, he had given all his attention. He was on the Commission which sat in 1845 in order to bring the monster into harness, and he had the chief hand in its report; but this report being rejected, he became disgusted with public life, and retired to more congenial occupation as Chairman of the Brighton Railway Company. In 1852 he was elected to Parliament for Wick, and he sat for that place until, having become a leader of those Liberal malcontents who in 1867 earned for themselves the name of Adullamites, he was rejected by his constituents at the general election of the following year, nor did he regain a seat till the present Session, when he was returned by his native Islands of Orkney. He is a moderate Liberal, with a determination to think for himself and to subordinate party-allegiance to his own convictions such as is unhappily too rare to avail in keeping immoderate leaders within due bounds. Nevertheless he believes in international arbitration and the Permissive Bill, and he must be fairly tractable, for he was once Financial Secretary to the Treasury for sixteen months, and Finance Minister of India for two years. Should the interests of Party ever allow of his being forgiven for his share in the formation of the Cave, the interests of the country would be served by his being employed again. But a Party does not easily forgive. Moreover Mr. Laing, although a good plain speaker of plain things, is not a graceful orator; and in a country ruled by the ears of majorities no abilities compensate for the want of smoothness of tongue."

Vanity Fair, 16 August 1873

10
Spy (Sir Leslie Ward) (1851-1922)
Mr Samuel Laing, MP
'The infant Samuel'
Signed
Watercolour and pencil with bodycolour, 12 x 6 ¾ inches
Illustrated: *Vanity Fair*, 16 August 1873, Statesmen no 151, 'The infant Samuel'

Coïdé (James Tissot) (1836-1902)
The Earl of Harrington

Charles Wyndham Stanhope (1809-1881) was the 7th Earl of Harrington. The grandson of the 3rd Earl of Harrington, the earldom had passed to him in 1866 following the death of his first cousin, Sydney Seymour Hyde Stanhope, who had died aged just 20 and childless.

'An Unexpected Earl'

"A few years ago there lived in the east of Ireland a gentleman with a large family a small income and prospects by no means brilliant. He bore names of historic memory, and came of one of those rich and powerful families founded in the halcyon days of Walpole when the bargain with the House of Brunswick was yet new and when the place of a minister was a mine of wealth. But he was the son of a younger son upon whose exposure the elder thrive, and as there seemed no prospect of his ever being anything else the family looked upon him as merely one of the accidental encumbrances of the estate. Out of his home he had not a large circle of friends; but at home he was loved and honoured, for he had all the qualities which entitle a man to the love and honour of his neighbours. His family, united in bonds of a rare affection were richly recompensed by it for the straitness of their circumstances. Living far away from the corruptions of cities they had retained that simplicity of manner which is the richest ornament of gentle men and women, and they passed their lives in such occupations as their income imposed and such relaxation as it permitted.

Suddenly, through a series of those unlikely events which only happen in real life, the poor gentleman became an unexpected Earl, the proprietor of a princely seat and the possessor of an almost princely income. From that time he and his family have been known to and caressed by Society. Prosperity commonly corrupts even those whom Adversity has elevated, but the great distinction of the Stanhopes is that their prosperity, sudden and great as it was, has left them still the same simple sympathetic family that they always were, so that they are of the few whose lives are open, clear and undimmed by intrigues social or otherwise, and whose intercourse is therefore grateful and refreshing. Lord Harrington, although became a Statesman by accident, is not a politician by practice, for he greatly prefers Music and Seafaring to Public Affairs, and his house at Cowes is the chosen centre for chamber-practice and nautical conversation. He is now sixty-four years of age and still delights in the Sea and the Fiddle."

Vanity Fair, 25 October 1873

11
Coïdé (James Tissot) (1836-1902)
The Earl of Harrington
'An Unexpected Earl'
Watercolour with bodycolour and pencil on tinted paper
12 x 7 ¼ inches
Provenance: Thomas Gibson Bowles; The John Franks Collection
Illustrated: *Vanity Fair*, 25 October 1873, Statesmen no 157,
'An Unexpected Earl'
Exhibited: 'James Tissot 1836-1902', Barbican, London;
Whitworth Art Gallery, Manchester, 1984;
Musee Du Petit Palais, Paris, November 1984-June 1985, no 43

The Earl of Desart

William Ulick O'Connor Cuffe (1845-1898), who succeeded to the title of 4th Earl of Desart at the age of 20, was an author of short stories and mystery thrillers who wrote fifteen novels across his career. His novels included *Beyond These Voices* (1870), *The Raid of the Detrimental* (1897) and *Love and Pride on an Iceberg: and Other Tales* (1887).

'Chesterfield Letters'

"The elder son of a poor titled Irish Family does not always find it an easy thing to make any great practical use of his ancestors; and, as often as not, has to rely upon himself more than upon his nobility to gain success of any kind in life. Lord Desart's family connections were nevertheless of some service to him, for at eleven years of age they made him page of honour to the Queen, in which capacity he distinguished himself according to his years by some escapades calculated to shock those who believe in the personal sanctity of Royalty. At seventeen, his domestic service at Court procured for him the usual reward of a Commission in the Guards, and he was so fortunate as to be sent almost immediately upon service more active than that of Windsor and London, for in the following year, he accompanied the Coldstreams to Canada. While there he sleighed, sported, and muffined, much to his own satisfaction, and he further distinguished himself and his regiment in the streets of Montreal by getting up the biggest fight with the police ever known. With two other peers and guardsmen at his side, he maintained on this occasion a Homeric struggle until overpowered by numbers and beaten into insensibility. Subsequently he returned to England, hunted for three seasons, married a young lady from Yorkshire, sent a challenge which was declined, and then went to live in his native wilds of Kilkenny. Finding there no other chance of a shindy, he took up the obstinate Father O'Keeffe and attended Magistrates' meetings. Then he began to cultivate Literature and the Drama. He twice appeared as a distinguished amateur on the boards in London, the editors of magazines began to know his fist, and two indifferent novels testified to the industry with which he kept it going. Still, life at Kilkenny, even when tempered with a half-season visit to London, is rather dull, and its dullness suggested to Lord Desart the conviction that the time had arrived for getting up a more striking shindy than any he had yet enjoyed. Wherefore he assumed the responsibility for 'the Chesterfield Letters of 1873,' written nobody knows by whom − unless indeed it were by Father O'Keeffe. It being fortunately a dull season, 'all London' became excited at finding some notorious impostures and swindles visited with satire and exemplified in certain fictitious characters, which were declared only thinly to disguise real individuals. Everybody said that 'something must be done,' and there seemed the most brilliant and certain prospect of a really good row. It ended however in the immortal journey of the three Colonels to Kilkenny, in order to demand not satisfaction by murderous arms, but Declaration in murdered English. They obtained, explained, and commented upon it in a manner which some persons thought proper, and thus deprived Lord Desart of all chance of immortalising either himself or any other person on Boulogne Sands.

Lord Desart is a great reader who has acquired a considerable knowledge of literature, a ready writer, and an energetic man, not disposed to echo the commonplaces or to agree with the common companions of Society. He will probably soon be a representative Irish Peer in the British Parliament, and in spite of his mere one-and-thirty years, he is likely to import into that august assembly a liveliness of debate and a novelty of ideas which will do it no harm."

Vanity Fair, 31 January 1874

12
APE (CARLO PELLEGRINI) (1839-1889)
The Earl of Desart
'Chesterfield Letters'
Signed
Watercolour and bodycolour on tinted paper
11 x 6 ¼ inches
Illustrated: *Vanity Fair*, 31 January 1874, Men of the Day no 79, 'Chesterfield Letters'

APE (CARLO PELLEGRINI) (1839-1889)
Sir Henry Drummond-Wolff, KCMG, MP

At the time of his appearance in *Vanity Fair*, Sir Henry Drummond-Wolff (1830-1908) had just become MP for Christchurch. He served in this role until 1880, when he became MP for Portsmouth. In 1885, he was sent to Constantinople and Egypt to negotiate as part of the Eastern Question and would serve as the British High Commissioner in Egypt from 1885 to 1887.

'Consular Chaplains'

"Provided by fortune with influential relatives, Drummond Wolff became a clerk in the Foreign Office at sixteen, and a lieutenant in the Norfolk Militia at twenty. He was then made Attaché at Florence, and was even for some time Chargé d'Affaires there before he was twenty-two. Subsequently he was Private Secretary to a Foreign Minister, and in 1859 he received what was held to be signal promotion by being appointed as Secretary to the High Commissioner of the Ionian Islands. The best things of the best kind of permanent official career were open to him, and certain to become his; but he was too active-minded, restless, and enterprising a man to be satisfied with any long and beaten though safe road to a merely respectable competency and position. He soon cast himself loose, therefore, from the official leading-strings, and began to embark in private enterprises of his own, and to contest seats in Parliament with an industry and cleverness only equalled by his want of success. He fell in succession at Dorchester, at Windsor, and at Christchurch before men certainly not his equals in ability; but having greatly interested himself in the welfare and prosperity of the Christchurch borough, having fixed his residence there, and created a neighbouring Spa, he was returned as in the due course of events at the last election by the borough of his choice. Great things were expected of him. He was known to be as ambitious as he was able, and with the knowledge he had acquired of the inner machinery of the Foreign Department, and the inclination he had shown to acknowledge no superior and to take an entirely independent course of his own, it was feared by the Conservative chiefs that he would be hard to lead. So indeed he has proved, and having inflicted upon the Foreign Office as represented by Lord Derby a signal defeat in the matter of consular chaplains, he is already regarded as dangerous, which is the sure preliminary of being held to be necessary. He speaks seldom and shortly, and therefore is always listened to; and he has a knack of discovering nasty questions which renders it a serious matter for him to speak at all. He has lived forty-four years in the world and has not yet learnt the art of saying nothing but what is absolutely safe; yet he has found it easier to be trusted than to trust. A cynic himself, yet with abundance of good temper, he looks upon men and things with an airy careless disbelief in their serious importance which is in itself a power. Witty and bright of converse and suspected of being a ready writer, he is much in favour as a guest with all who know him; and were he ever to embark in other than political pursuits, his brilliant and persuasive speech would win any amount of support for any undertaking he might patronise."

Vanity Fair, 5 September 1874

13
APE (CARLO PELLEGRINI) (1839-1889)
Sir Henry Drummond-Wolff, KCMG, MP
'Consular Chaplains'
Signed
Inscribed 'Drummond Wolff' and dated '5 Sept 74' on reverse
Watercolour
12 x 7 inches
Illustrated: *Vanity Fair*, 5 September 1874, Statesmen no 184, 'Consular Chaplains'

APE (CARLO PELLEGRINI) (1839-1889)
Sir William Augustus Fraser, of Morar, Bart, MP

A staunch Conservative, Sir William Augustus Fraser became a familiar figure at the Carlton Club, where he was known for his story-telling about the Duke of Wellington and Waterloo, as his father Colonel Sir John James Fraser, had been on the staff at Waterloo. He gradually became an authority on the Duke of Wellington and published two volumes of anecdotes, *Words on Wellington* (1889), followed by *The Waterloo Ball* (1897). A great admirer of Benjamin Disraeli and Napoleon III, he also published the works *Disraeli and his Day* (1891), *Hic et ubique* (1893), and *Napoleon III* (1896). As a Conservative, Fraser sat as MP for Barnstaple from 1857 to 1859, Ludlow from 1863 to 1865 and Kidderminster from 1874 to 1880.

'The Sanitary'

"Coming of a soldier-like Scotch race and finding himself already a baronet when still a boy, Sir William Fraser indulged the family lust for fighting by entering the Life Guards, and before he had ceased to be a young man he had sought distinction as Member of Parliament for Barnstaple. Among the Commons he soon became known for repeating sharp epigrams and smart sentences; yet ten years ago he retired from statesmanship to devote himself more entirely to his duty as one of the Queen's Body Guard for Scotland, and to his destiny as a poet and collector of curiosities.
A considerable sensation was created among those who saw it by the printing of the collected verses of the Knight of Morar, who was at once accepted not only as a manipulator of feet but also as a professor of verse and a richly-endowed student of all the inspired who had gone before him. He has now once again, at the more matured age of eight-and-forty, returned to Parliament; and from the bent of his mind and the reputation he has already made in connection with sewers, he is looked to as the sanitary reformer and general guardian of the Metropolis. For indeed he is a thorough London man. Well acquainted, well liked, picturesque in appearance, remarkable for readiness of converse and store of anecdote, he is received with equal pleasure and satisfaction by all the ladies, and is yet on the best terms with all the men of the town. He has the quality of doing things thoroughly, and whether it be a question of typography, the origin of a quotation, or the authenticity and true version of a received history that is on hand, he is always found carefully provided with the most correct canons of taste and the most inaccessible sources of information. Tracing his genealogy as far back as the tenth century, from Oliver the thirteenth Thane of Man, and being an archaeologist of some pretensions, he is yet quite unaffected and thoroughly accessible; and he has the most complete collection of caricatures in England."

Vanity Fair, 9 January 1875

14
APE (CARLO PELLEGRINI) (1839-1889)
Sir William Augustus Fraser, of Morar, Bart, MP
'The Sanitary'
Inscribed 'Sir W Fraser'
Pencil
13 ¼ x 9 inches
Illustrated: Preliminary drawing for *Vanity Fair*, 9 January 1875, Statesmen no 192, 'The Sanitary'

APE (CARLO PELLEGRINI) (1839-1889)
The Right Hon Sir John Charles Dalrymple Hay, Bart, MP

Sir John Charles Dalrymple Hay (1821-1912) was a naval officer and politician. He joined the navy in 1834 as a 13 year old and served on numerous ships, including as captain of the HMS Victory. In 1866, he was promoted to rear admiral, the same year he was appointed junior naval lord in the Derby ministry. On 1 March 1870, Hay was placed on the list of officers to be retired under the reform introduced by the Liberal first lord, Hugh Childers. Though he protested this decision, it was upheld by the Prime Minister Benjamin Disraeli. As a politician, Hay sat as Conservative MP for Wakefield from 1862 to 1865 and for Stamford from 1866 to 1880.

'The Retired List'

"The elder son of a second baronet, coming of an old Scottish family, Sir John Hay was wisely sent into the Navy at thirteen, served with bravery and distinction in all parts of the world, and seemed destined to the most brilliant career and the highest kind of reputation that a British sailor need desire. But at forty he left sailorising to begin politics, and being brought into the House of Commons for Wakefield, he was received as a naval authority and soon made a Lord of the Admiralty. When his Party went out in 1868 he found himself without sufficient employment, and was so ill advised as to embark in commercial operations, in the belief that a poor gentleman might take part in such with safety as well as with profit. The result has been that although his honour has remained unquestioned, his judgment and information have been found in fault, and that he has been made to suffer much criticism and great losses, for which his only consolation can be the consciousness of the rectitude of this purposes. It was but last year he was made a Privy Councillor, and seemed certain to play an important part in the affairs of the country; and were this not the case it would be impossible not to feel sympathy and regret for the sailor who at his age of fifty-four is found to have been made so completely the dupe of designing persons. Sir John is a Vice-Admiral on the retired list."

Vanity Fair, 12 June 1875

15
APE (CARLO PELLEGRINI) (1839-1889)
The Right Hon Sir John Charles Dalrymple Hay, Bart, MP
'The Retired List'
Signed
Watercolour and bodycolour on tinted paper
12 x 7 inches
Provenance: Thomas Gibson Bowles;
The John Franks Collection
Illustrated: *Vanity Fair*, 12 June 1875, Statesmen no. 205, 'The Retired List'
Exhibited: 'In Vanity Fair', Stanford University, San Francisco, September-November 1980; 'Vanity Fair 1869-1914', Church Farm House Museum, Hendon, September-December 1983

APE (CARLO PELLEGRINI) (1839-1889)
Prince Edward of Saxe-Weimar

The son of Duke Bernard of Saxe-Weimar-Eisenach and Princess Ada, Prince Edward was born William Augustus Edward at Bushey Park, home of the Duke of Clarence (later William IV), and was chiefly brought up in England by the Duke's wife, Queen Adelaide. As a child, he was a playfellow and friend of Queen Victoria and remained close to her throughout his life. Having been naturalised, Edward went to Sandhurst and entered the army in 1841. He served with distinction in the Crimea, seeing action at Alma, Bakalava and during the siege of Sevastopol. For his services he was awarded the CB, the Légion d'honneur and the Medjidie. He was appointed brevet colonel and aide-de-camp to Queen Victoria on 5 October 1855, and retained the position until 22 February 1869, when he was promoted major general. At the time of his portrait in *Vanity Fair*, Edward was commanding the home district. On 6 July 1877 he became lieutenant general and in 1878 he was appointed Colonel of the 10th (North Lincolnshire) regiment, and in November 1879 became general. From October 1885 to September 1890 he commanded the forces in Ireland. From 1888 he was Colonel-in-Chief of the 1st Life Guards, and as such was gold stick-in-waiting to the queen. He retired on 11 October 1890.

'Guards'

"Prince Edward is a remarkable instance of the success which may be achieved by steady devotion to and decent and popular conduct in the profession of arms even by a person of exalted rank. In Saxe-Weimar-Eisenach he would have held but an indifferently good position, and would probably not have made for himself any great military name. But although he has been called a foreign general, he was born fifty-one years ago at Bushy Park, and went to Sandhurst, where 'gentleman-cadet Saxe-Weimar' soon became known to his comrades as a good fellow, giving himself no airs and not more devoted to the science of the shop than is held to be desirable. In his studies he achieved no very brilliant success, but on entering the Grenadier Guards and becoming morganatically married to a Lennox, his merits were at once recognised. He had an early opportunity of seeing service in the Crimea, where he showed courage and coolness, and was wounded in the trenches. So that he was promoted with all due rapidity, and four years ago was made a Major-General and appointed to the command of the London district. Since then he has continually been employed as the commander of Brigades or of Divisions at reviews and manœuvres not prevented by providential weather, and the remarks he makes upon such occasions are treasured up as the best things in the traditions of the British army. He is popular among Guardsmen who appreciate his good comradeship, and are thankful to have over them a chief neither of devouring activity nor wedded to the severer views of smart soldiership. He always appears to be frank and straightforward; his nickname bears testimony to the appreciation in which he is held by his fellow-soldiers; he is on the best of terms with the Field-Marshal Commanding-in-Chief; and his rapid rise in his profession shows how much better judges of ability there are at the Horse Guards than are to be found among those who, being less fortunate than the Prince, are disposed to criticise his success."

Vanity Fair, 30 October 1875

16
APE (CARLO PELLEGRINI) (1839-1889)
Prince Edward of Saxe-Weimar
'Guards'
Watercolour and bodycolour with pencil
11 ¾ x 6 ¾ inches
Provenance: Thomas Gibson Bowles; Sale. Christie's, London, Original Drawings For *Vanity Fair*; 5-8 March 1912, Lot 691 (3 Gns. To Craig); Stanley Jackson; John Franks, From The Collection of Original Watercolours For *Vanity Fair*
Illustrated: *Vanity Fair*, 30 October 1875, Men of the Day no 114, 'Guards'
Exhibited: Hendon, Church Farm House Museum, Vanity Fair 1869-1914, September-December, 1983

Greece

"His Majesty George I, King of Greece, is like his Kingdom, an accident. Fourteen years ago the crown of Greece went a-begging. It had successively been offered to and refused by the Duke of Edinburgh and the Duke Ernest of Saxe-Coburg-Gotha, when it occurred to so some astute persons that there was in the North a family which had recently been taken under the protection of the Powers and protocolised into a place not hitherto belonging to it. For by the Treaty of May 1852, the claims of the House of Augustenburg and three others had been set aside, and the family of Schleswig-Holstein Sonderburg Glücksburg had been designated as the heirs to Denmark and the Duchies-the rights, however, of the line of Holstein-Gottor, represented by the Emperor of Russia, being reserved. A scion of this House seemed therefore a desirable Sovereign for Greece, and from being a Danish Admiral Prince George, then a lad of eighteen, was brought to the Greek throne. Four years later he married the Grand-Duchess Olga, niece of the Emperor Alexander, and thus, as it was presumed, finally assured to his kingdom the protection of Russia, which protection, however, was immediately found insufficient to enable it to wrest Crete from the Turk. The advent of Queen Olga, however, caused, and still causes, the Court of Greece to be one of the most stuck-up and tiresome in Europe; and the countenance of his Imperial relative has not availed to prevent the reign of this unfortunate young man from being one continued series of troubles and anxieties, which have repeatedly driven him to the verge of abdication, Although now one and thirty, he is still but a boy – a good boy, indeed, but poorly brought up, and without anything like sufficient notions of policy to enable him to play any other part than that of an instrument in the destinies of his adopted country. The best thing that can be said of him is, that he is the brother of the Princess of Wales."

Vanity Fair, 21 October 1876

SPY (SIR LESLIE WARD) (1851-1922)
HM Christian William Ferdinand Adolphus George, King of Greece

Spy's caricature of King George is a reminder of British, and generally international, involvement in the governance of Greece following its independence from the Ottoman Empire in 1830. At the London Conference in 1832, The 'Great Powers' – Britain, France and Russia – recognised the country's autonomy and established a monarchy in Greece under the Bavarian prince, Otto. He reigned for 30 years, but became increasingly unpopular with native Greek politicians, and was deposed in 1862. He was replaced at the suggestion of the Great Powers by the 17 year old Danish prince, William (1845-1913). He was elected the King of the Hellenes in 1863, and took the regnal name of George. At his urging, Greece adopted a more democratic constitution, and greatly developed its parliamentary process.

In the same year, his sister, Alexandria, married (Albert) Edward, the Prince of Wales and future Edward VII. These personal bonds further strengthened relations between Britain and Greece, and helped maintain George's reputation among the British people, as exemplified by Spy's gentle caricature, which was published in 1876.

During the nineteenth century there was a desire in Greek politics to unify all areas that had been historically inhabited by the ethnically Greek people. So, in 1897, the Greek population of Crete rose up against its Ottoman rulers, and the Greek Prime Minister, Theodoros Diligiannis, mobilised troops, which invaded Crete and crossed the Macedonian border into the Ottoman Empire. When Greece lost the war that followed, King George considered abdicating. However, when he survived an assassination attempt in 1898, his subjects began to hold him in greater esteem. In 1901, on the death of Queen Victoria he became the second-longest-reigning monarch in Europe.

In 1912, the Kingdom of Montenegro declared war against the Ottoman Empire, Crown Prince Constantine led the victorious Greek forces in support of the Ottoman Empire, in what became known as the First Balkan War. George planned to abdicate in favour of his son immediately after the celebration of his Golden Jubilee in October 1913. However, while walking in Thessaloniki on 18 March 1913, he was assassinated by the anarchist, Alexandros Schinas. Constantine succeeded to the throne.

17
SPY (SIR LESLIE WARD) (1851-1922)
H.M. Christian William Ferdinand Adolphus George, King of Greece
'Greece'
Signed
Watercolour and bodycolour with ink on tinted paper
12 x 7 ¼ inches
Illustrated: *Vanity Fair*, 21 October 1876, Sovereigns no 12, 'Greece'

SPY (SIR LESLIE WARD) (1851-1922)
Colonel Charles Napier Sturt

Charles Napier Sturt (1832-1886) was Conservative MP for Dorchester in the period 1856-74. As a lieutenant-colonel in the Grenadier Guards, he was severely wounded in 1854 at the Battle of Inkerman, during the Crimean War.

'A Younger Son'

"Napier Sturt is the younger son of an ancient, and honourable Dorsetshire family; the name of which has recently been with much labour regilt, without being improved, by its eldest possessor. Born a short four-and-forty years ago, he was sent to Harrow, and thence into the Grenadier Guards, in which distinguished regiment he served in the Crimea, and has since pursued a successful career of Society and soldiering, winning at once great approbation from his military superiors and the greatest good-will of his fellow-officers and civilian associates. As a soldier, his pre-eminent humility and reverence for discipline have been greatly remarked. He has never been known to ruffle the feathers even of a Brigadier; and the Duke of Cambridge, with that playful badinage which is the sole privilege of Commanding-in-chief, has more than once borne testimony to his deferential qualities by ironically pronouncing him 'the most insubordinate officer in the British Army.' With such a claim to promotion, it is natural that he should be looked upon as the future Adjutant-General; but in the meantime he is devoted to sport of all kinds, and wherever amusing and profitable Society is to be found, there is he to be found also. In truth, he knows well-nigh everybody and everything that is necessary to be known in London; he has a remarkable instinct for perceiving the real instead of being misled as most are by the apparent importance of bodies and things; and withal he possesses so much tact, and shows so much energy in utilising them, that, if he had not been a soldier, he would assuredly have made a good diplomat.

Poor, but honest, he avoids display and glories in penury. He is reported to have written for the public, which is not impossible, since in private he possesses a handy knack of laconic statement and terse epigram. He was in Parliament for seventeen years as member for Dorchester, but his political opinions, which are Conservative tempered by Liberalism, never so violently influenced him as to cause him to withdraw from his friends and his regiment the countenance and support he had been accustomed to extend to them. A subscription is on foot to present him with a watch and chain."

Vanity Fair, 25 November 1876

18
SPY (SIR LESLIE WARD) (1851-1922)
Colonel Charles Napier Sturt
'A Younger Son'
Signed
Watercolour with bodycolour on tinted paper
12 x 7 ¼ inches
Illustrated: *Vanity Fair*, 25 November 1876, Men of the Day no 142,
'A Younger Son'

SPY (SIR LESLIE WARD) (1851-1922)
Lord Kensington, MP

William Edwardes (1835-1896) was Liberal MP for Haverfordwest in Pembrokeshire during the period 1868-85. Though succeeding to the title of Baron Kensington in the Peerage of Ireland in 1872, he remained in the House of Commons, as a whip, a member of the Privy Council and, latterly, Comptroller of the Household (1880-85). Created 1st Baron Kensington in the Peerage of the United Kingdom in 1886, he then entered the House of Lords, and acted as its Liberal Chef Whip in 1892-96.

'A Whip'

"Three generations ago there was a Lord Kensington of great possessions who was addicted to the then fashionable vice of gambling. On one occasion he staked the whole of that estate now known as Holland Park, and now worth probably a million of money, against ten thousand pounds, and, having lost it, left his family with an inconsiderable number of acres in Kensington which appeared unlikely ever to be of any value. His son and grandson were poor men; but the Metropolitan Railway having come into existence, the unregarded land of the family has enormously increased in value, and the present Lord Kensington is the possessor of a very handsome peer's income, as well as the inheritor of family traditions of a Welsh ancestry extending beyond the limits of history.

Born three-and-forty years ago, he was sent to Eton, and into the Coldstream Guards, adopted Liberal opinions and was elected a Member of Parliament for Haverfordwest when three-and-thirty. Since that time he has addressed himself to Parliamentary work with much industry, and though he has not made himself known as an orator, his knowledge of the House is much relied upon by his chiefs, so that they have made him a Whip of the Party. He is well-mannered, well-known, well-liked, and a gentleman."

Vanity Fair, 7 September 1878

19
SPY (SIR LESLIE WARD) (1851-1922)
Lord Kensington, MP
'A Whip'
Signed
Ink and watercolour with bodycolour and pencil
13 ¼ x 7 ¾ inches
Illustrated: *Vanity Fair*, 7 September 1878, Statesmen no 281, 'A Whip'

Sir Leslie Ward, RP (1851-1922)
Sir George Bowyer, Bart, MP

Trained as a lawyer, George Bowyer (1811-1883) was called to the bar at Middle Temple in June 1839, the same month he was awarded an honorary MA from Oxford, and was admitted as a member of Lincoln's Inn in 1845. In 1841, he had established his reputation as a constitutional lawyer with the publication of *The English Constitution: a Popular Commentary on the Constitutional Laws of England*. In 1850, he converted to Roman Catholicism and became an active spokesman for the Catholic church on legal and constitutional questions. As a defender of Catholic causes in Parliament, he was made a knight commander of the Order of Pius IX. He was elected MP for Dundalk, County Louth, in 1852, and for County Wexford in 1874.

'The Knight of Malta'

"Sir George Bowyer is the worthy representative of a fine old English family, which received a baronetcy over two hundred years ago. At twenty-eight he became a barrister, at thirty-nine a Roman Catholic, and at forty-one a Member of Parliament. For the last twenty years he has been well known in public life as a fine writer, a good constitutional lawyer, and the professed partisan of the Pope. He is not an orator, but his speeches are full of good matter, and always give evidence of research and thought. He is, moreover, honest and a gentleman, and he is much esteemed even by those who do not attach great importance to his political judgment. He is seven and sixty years of age, and a Knight of Malta."

Vanity Fair, 18 January 1879

20
Sir Leslie Ward, RP (1851-1922)
Sir George Bowyer, Bart, MP
'The Knight of Malta'
Signed
Watercolour and bodycolour on tinted paper
12 x 7 inches
Illustrated: *Vanity Fair*, 18 January 1879, Statesmen no 293,
'The Knight of Malta'

SPY (SIR LESLIE WARD) (1851-1922)
Viscount Castlereagh, MP

In 1878, the year before his appearance in *Vanity Fair*, Charles Stewart Vane-Tempest (1852-1915) had just returned as MP for the Irish seat of County Down. He was styled as Viscount Castlereagh until 1884, when he succeeded his father as Marquess of Londonderry. In July 1886, he was appointed Viceroy of Ireland in Lord Salisbury's government.

'C'

"Lord Castlereagh is not yet twenty-seven, and he has already fought three of the most expensive contested elections of this generation, the last of which resulted in his being returned to Parliament for Co. Down, and in his moving the Address with much modesty and good taste. The son of an affectionate father, he was sent to Eton and Oxford, was made a Volunteer and a Conservative, and three years ago married a beautiful and charming wife. He has very good manners; he is a fair rider to hounds, is fond of horses, and is known as 'C' to all the smarter sort. He has good natural talents, no excessive amount of application, and none of that devouring ambition which wears men out before their time. His prospects are of the most brilliant kind, and if he should show a disposition to be so, he will certainly become one of the subaltern officers of that Conservative Party which his father has done so much to support."

Vanity Fair, 7 June 1879

21
SPY (SIR LESLIE WARD) (1851-1922)
Viscount Castlereagh, MP
'C'
Signed
Watercolour and bodycolour with ink
12 x 7 inches
Illustrated: *Vanity Fair*, 7 June 1879, Statesmen no 305, 'C'

Ape (Carlo Pellegrini) (1839-1889)
Lord Headley

Sir Charles Mark Allanson Winn (1845-1913) was educated at Harrow and University College, Oxford. As a young man, it appears that he travelled to France and Prussia to observe the Franco-Prussian War of 1870-1871 as a non-combatant, and wrote about his experiences. He succeeded his father as the 4th Lord Headley, Baron Allanson and Winn of Aghadoe, County Kerry in July 1877. Following his appearance in *Vanity Fair*, he was appointed Captain of the Honorable Artillery Company in 1881, a post he held until 1885. He was appointed Representative Peer in Ireland in 1883 and served as Deputy Lieutenant of County Kerry.

'A loyal Irishman'

"When a candidate was wanted for a great London borough the managers of the Conservative Party probably thought that at the present juncture a loyal Irishman would be, if not exactly a novelty, still sufficiently rare to be an interesting object. So Sir Charles Mark Allanson Winn, Baron Headley, stood for Marylebone.

Although a Welshman by origin, Lord Headley is a true Irishman by virtue of birth and of residence, and also of that spirit of combativeness which makes him so good a representative of militant Conservatism. From Harrow he went to Oxford, from Oxford to matrimony, and thence to a Captaincy in the Kerry Militia. But such civilian soldiering was not sufficient for the scion of the fiery old Wynnes of Gwydir; and the Franco-German War saw him earning golden opinions amongst the grizzled warriors who fought under General von Göben and who made havoc of the tactics of Generals Faidherbe and Chanzy. Not content however with his reputation for coolness under fire, and for all other qualities required by a non-combatant who is running the risk of death as a holiday pastime, he came home to prove his ability as an author; and his book called 'What I Saw of the War,' which was the first published on the subject, bears testimony to his fitness to record the stirring scenes in which he had taken part.

For the rest, Lord Headley has political ability and shrewdness, is imbued with the old-fashioned idea of honour, and is so generous a foe that he would tenderly pick up a defeated opponent, if only for the pleasure of knocking him down again."

Vanity Fair, 3 April 1880

22
Ape (Carlo Pellegrini) (1839-1889)
Lord Headley
'A loyal Irishman'
Signed
Watercolour with bodycolour
12 x 7 inches
Illustrated: *Vanity Fair*, **3 April 1880, Men of the Day no 22,**
'A loyal Irishman'

Théobald Chartran (1849-1907)
M. Victorien Sardou

Born in Paris, Victorien Sardou (1831-1908) was a playwright and, along with Alexandre Dumas and Émile Augier, one of the leading dramatists of the French stage in the nineteenth-century. With Augier, he is best-known as a developer of the dramatic genre known as the 'well-made play'. He enjoyed a highly successful career, with works such as *Madame Sans-Gêne* (1893), which is still performed today, and *La Tosca* (1897), upon which Puccini's *Tosca* (1900) was based. Despite his success, his work was belittled as 'Sardoodledom' in an 1895 article by George Bernard Shaw. He was awarded the Légion d'honneur in 1863, and was elected to the Académie Française in 1877.

'Ficelle dramatique'

"The son of a Professor, M. Victorien Sardou was born nine-and-forty years ago. He studied medicine, which he abandoned for history, gaining a living the while by giving lessons in philosophy and mathematics. At twenty-three he wrote a play and got it acted. It was a dismal failure; but having married at twenty-seven into the theatrical world, he tried again, and with so much good fortune that he is now perhaps the most popular and successful play-writer in France. 'Les Pattes de Mouche,' 'Les Ganaches,' 'Nos Intimes,' 'Les Vieux Garçons,' 'La famille Benoiton,' 'Nos bons Villageois,' and 'Fernande' are some of the best of his plays, and they are all excellent. He is a master of dramatic construction and of that trick of the dramatic art which is known as 'ficelle.' His dialogue is at once brilliant and natural. He has been convicted of plagiarism and decorated with the Legion of Honour."

Vanity Fair, 25 December 1880

23
Théobald Chartran (1849-1907)
M. Victorien Sardou
'Ficelle dramatique'
Signed with monogram
Watercolour and bodycolour on tinted paper
12 ¼ x 7 ¼ inches
Illustrated: *Vanity Fair,* 25 December 1880, Men of the Day no 235, 'Ficelle dramatique'

APE (CARLO PELLEGRINI) (1839-1889)
Colonel Lewis Guy Phillips

After an education at Eton and Christchurch College, Oxford, where he became fluent in several languages including Ancient and Modern Greek, German, Italian and French, Lewis Guy Phillips (1831-1887) opted for a career in the military, joining the 1st Battalion Grenadier Guards in 1859. On 1 December 1861, Phillips was dispatched to Canada as part of a contingent sent to reinforce the British Garrison stationed there during the American Civil War.

Eager to observe the action of the Civil War and with sympathies towards the Confederate cause, Phillips and another soldier, Captain Edward Wynne, were granted a leave of absence in October 1862 and, with the help of a Confederate sympathiser in Baltimore, were smuggled through the lines into Virginia. Phillips was able to access the headquarters of General Robert E Lee and served as an aide-de-camp during the Battle of Fredericksburg in December 1862. Following the battle he was able to return to Canada and continued to serve in Montreal before returning to England in December 1864. In 1867 he was promoted to lieutenant colonel and retired in 1885 with the honorary rank of major general.

'Order at Wimbledon'

"Some twenty-five years ago a tall youth came from Eton to Christchurch with the reputation of being a good cricketer, a wonderful runner, and a marvellous boxer. While at College he kept up his credit in these matters, and added to them much distinction as what used to be called an 'elegant classic'. Although blessed with a knowledge of modern tongues that would have benefited the Diplomatic Service, he chose the Army as a serious profession; and – Fortune having denied him the opportunity of ever fighting the Queen's enemies – he has managed to smell powder in the American War of Secession, serving on one occasion – during the battle of Fredericksburg – as a volunteer aide-de-camp to General Lee. Colonel Phillips was ten years since chosen to keep order at Wimbledon as Camp-Commandant, and has proved that moral suasion is as powerful, when administered with tact and firmness, as the Articles of War. He is an acute bibliophile, and has collected many thousand wonderful volumes. He has been offered posts of honour abroad, but has preferred the calm pleasures of soldiering at St James's. He has never broken the eleventh commandment, and, possibly for this reason, he has never been married."

Vanity Fair, 24 June 1880

24
APE (CARLO PELLEGRINI) (1839-1889)
Colonel Lewis Guy Phillips
'Order at Wimbledon'
Signed
Watercolour and bodycolour with ink on tinted paper
12 x 7 ¼ inches
Provenance: Thomas Gibson Bowles;
The John Franks Collection
Illustrated: *Vanity Fair*, 24 June 1880, Men of the Day no 229,
'Order at Wimbledon'

Spy (Sir Leslie Ward) (1851-1922)
The Earl of Winchilsea and Nottingham

The 11th Earl of Winchilsea and 6th Earl of Nottingham, George James Finch-Hatton was elected MP for Northamptonshire North from 1837 to 1841, before succeeding his father to the earldom in 1858 and entering the House of Lords. The earl entered into financial difficulties during the 1860s, was forced to vacate the family estate of Eastwell Park, which was let to the Duke of Abercorn, and was declared bankrupt in 1870.

'Youth'

"Sixty five years ago there was born to the ancient house of Finch-Hatton an heir; and an heir moreover who, as time moved on, appeared likely to make the name illustrious in the annals of England.

George James Viscount Maidstone excelled in classics at Oxford, wrote capital political squibs in London, married a beautiful Paget, sat in Parliament for Northamptonshire, and even bearded, and bearded successfully, the demagogue O'Connell in all his glory. Whether as 'John Davis' the lampoonist, as the elegant scholar, or as the witty companion, he was popular wherever he went, and it was predicted of him that he would do great things.

But, perhaps because he seems to have learned the secret of perpetual youth, he has not begun to do the great things yet. He has a wonderful knowledge of racing, and, indeed, of most things under the sun; he can write verses that will scan, and will not suffer a false quantity from others, he dresses beautifully, is the soul of honour, and knows how to bear misfortune like a gentleman. His motto very fitly is, 'Nil conscire sibi.'"

Vanity Fair, 2 October 1880

25
Spy (Sir Leslie Ward) (1851-1922)
The Earl of Winchilsea and Nottingham
'Youth'
Signed
Watercolour and bodycolour with pencil on tinted paper
14 x 10 inches
Illustrated: *Vanity Fair*, 2 October 1880, Statesmen no 341, 'Youth'

APE (CARLO PELLEGRINI) (1839-1889)
Sir John George Tollemache Sinclair, Bart, MP

Scottish landowner Sir John Sinclair (1825-1912) was a Liberal Politician who sat in the House of Commons as MP for Caithness between 1869 and 1885.

'A Poet'

"The northernmost rock of Scotland is his home. He was born four-and-sixty years ago; he was a page of Queen Adelaide's' and he developed into an officer of the Scots Fusiliers. But the career of arms did not suffice for a man of his abilities and consequence. He retired therefore and devoted himself to poetry, politics, and the maintenance of his social position. At twenty-six he essayed to represent Caithness-shire; and at forty-five he succeeded in being returned for it to a Parliament which he has now embellished for eleven years.

As a political power he has not been duly recognised; as a statesman he has not been appreciated. During the troubles between Russia and Turkey he printed and published, at his own expense, a large book to prove that Russia was right and ought to be supported by England, and that Mr Gladstone and the Duke of Argyll were the saviours of their country. But the Emperor of Russia took no notice of him, and the Duke of Argyll failed to return his visit. This made him understand the unworthiness of the men whom he had supported, and his natural indignation and repentance of his unappreciated efforts have been vented in verses of a moving character. For Sir Tollemache is a poet. He has written epigrams, madrigals, and idylls both in French and in English, which, with the profusion of a generous nature, he imparts to all who know him. His poetry is indeed of no common order, and is therefore beyond the understanding of the present generation, but the day will come when it will be appraised at its true value. He is forgiving and amiable, and the father of a most charming and beautiful daughter."

Vanity Fair, 16 October 1880

26
Ape (Carlo Pellegrini) (1839-1889)
Sir John George Tollemache Sinclair, Bart, MP
'A Poet'
Signed
Watercolour and bodycolour with pencil
12 ½ x 7 inches
Provenance: Thomas Gibson Bowles;
The John Franks Collection
Illustrated: *Vanity Fair*, 16 October 1880, Statesmen no 343, 'A Poet'
Exhibited: 'Vanity Fair 1869-1914', Church Farm House Museum, Hendon, September-December 1983

SPY (SIR LESLIE WARD) (1851-1922)
General Lord Chelmsford, GCB

Frederic Augustus Thesiger (1827-1905) was an army officer who served for sixteen years in India before being made major general in 1877. The following year he was selected as general officer in South Africa and charged with ending the Cape Frontier War. Under his command, the British forces were defeated at the Battle of Isandlwana (also known as Isandula), for which Chelmsford suffered strong criticism back in Britain.

'Isandula'

"Some generations ago a German named Thesiger came from Saxony to England and married an Englishwoman. Then Thesigers began to determine to the Customs, the Army, and the Navy. Finally, Frederick Thesiger went into Law and Conservatism, got made Attorney-General by Sir Robert Peel, and in due course of time became Lord Chancellor and Baron Chelmsford. But the Baron outlived the reputation of the Attorney-General, and when he was verging towards four-score he was set aside by the Conservative leaders for the younger Lord Cairns. The result was that the Thesiger family was held to have acquired, from the passing over of its head, a special claim to be 'got on.'

The present and second Baron Chelmsford was at that time the eldest son and heir-apparent of the ex-Chancellor. He was in the Army, and he became an object of special interest to the Commander-in-Chief and the rest of the Royal Family. In 1867 he was sent with Lord Napier as Deputy-Adjutant-General to Abyssinia, where he exerted himself more successfully in suggesting his own idea of his own importance than in establishing a reputation for accuracy. But he still grew in favour with the Court and the Horse Guards. He became distinguished as an able player of Kriegspiel. He was appointed Aide-de-camp to the Queen. He was installed in the command of an infantry brigade at Aldershot, and when in 1878 things began to look serious in South Africa he was sent out to the Cape as Commander-in-Chief and Lieutenant-Governor. In October, 1878, finding that he would probably be ordered to invade Zululand, he carefully inspected the borders of that country, and in November he reported that in a few weeks he should be ready to enter it. Accordingly he did enter it in January, 1879, and encamped at Isandula. On the 22nd January, hearing that the enemy had been found, he left his camp in the charge of Colonel Pulleine, with orders to 'defend it,' but without having either ascertained whether there was any special danger to it, or having given any specific orders to meet such a danger. He had scarcely got well away from the camp before – at nine in the morning – he received a note from Colonel Pulleine announcing that fighting was going on hard by the camp. He sent an officer to the top of a hill with a telescope, and 'having no cause to feel any anxiety about the safety of the camp,' wandered on, looking into dongas and ditches for the Zulus. Meantime the Zulus had fallen upon his camp in overwhelming numbers, and had massacred nearly every soul therein, to the number of over fourteen hundred men. When Lord Chelmsford returned in the evening from his wanderings he found a shambles instead of a camp. He was horror-stricken and panic-stricken. He scuttled away with the remains of his army before it was light the next morning, and without waiting to see if by chance any of the devoted defenders of the camp yet remained alive. Having got to a safe distance, he wrote a despatch declaring the disaster to be 'to me almost incomprehensible,' and conveying that it arose through the men not having had the courage to 'keep their faces to the enemy.'

Upon the first news of Isandula arriving in England the Queen sent a precipitate telegram to Lord Chelmsford expressive of condolence and confidence. This was as unfortunate as it was premature; for it has been made abundantly clear by Lord Chelmsford's own despatches that he was not wholly entitled to confidence, and that the condolence should have been reserved for those who were committed to his leadership. The great player of Kriegspiel having been outwitted, out-manœuvred, and beaten in strategy and in tactics by ignorant savages, began to whimper. He complained of 'the strain of prolonged anxiety and exertion, physical and mental.' In the involved and floundering language of a distraught man he begged to be relieved of that strain. All too tardily, and after having been allowed an entirely insufficient chance to whitewash himself by being present at the Battle of Ulundi, he was so relieved, and returned to England to be caressed by the Court and the Horse Guards, and to assume the position of a General who had suffered the most disgraceful defeat, in British annals.

Lord Chelmsford is not a bad man. He is industrious and conscientious so far as his lights guide him, But Nature has refused to him the qualities of a great captain. He has suffered much and is entitled to a certain commiseration. But he has been ill-served by Fate and his friends; and he has not yet understood that the duty of a General who has sacrificed an army and has yet escaped the fate of Byng, and even a trial by court-martial, is to avoid the public gaze. For he is still ready to return thanks for the Army."

Vanity Fair, 3 September 1880

27
SPY (SIR LESLIE WARD) (1851-1922)
General Lord Chelmsford, GCB
'Isandula'
Signed
Watercolour and bodycolour
12 x 7 ½ inches
Illustrated: *Vanity Fair*, 3 September 1881,
Statesmen no 370, 'Isandula'

SPY (SIR LESLIE WARD) (1851-1922)
The Duke of Norfolk

The fifteenth Duke of Norfolk, Henry Fitzalan-Howard (1847-1917), was a deeply religious man who succeeded his father as duke at the age of 13. In 1887 he was sent by Queen Victoria as a special envoy to Pope Leo XIII and maintained close relations with the papacy throughout his life. He developed an intense interest in public ceremonies and would be responsible for managing the funerals of both William Gladstone and Queen Victoria.

'Our Little Duke'

"Henry Fitzalan-Howard, fifteenth Duke of Norfolk, Earl of Arundel, Surrey, and Norfolk, Baron Fitzalan, Clun, Oswaldestrie and Maltravers, Premier Duke, Hereditary Earl Marshal and Chief Butler of England, stands next to the Blook Royal in dignity. The splendid name and traditions of his house are found on every page of English history for nigh six hundred years, and he who now bears them is a most admirably well-regulated and worthy young man, who may one day play a personal part in the destinies of this country other than that of bearing the wand of his inherited office. He is not a genius, and will never be a leader of men; but he is thoroughly honest and good, generous to the poor, and a devout Roman Catholic known to his co-religionists as 'our Little Duke.' Though naturally indolent, he conscientiously works several hours every day in answering letters of business and the charitable appeals to which he is condemned as one of the richest men in the country. Withal he takes up both in political and religious matters strong and decided views of his own, to which he adheres with much tenacity; and being essentially conservative in his notions, he even seemed to disapprove the disestablishment of the Anglican Church in Ireland, and to doubt whether any good could come out of a measure apparently tending to strengthen the Liberal Party as much as to emancipate the Roman Catholics. He is of course much courted and influenced by his priests, yet it was in direct opposition to the wishes of the chiefs of the Roman Catholic party (who would have preferred to see the money spent in other ways) that he built the splendid church at Arundel, which overtops his adjacent castle, as a monument to the memory of his father and a record of his own taste for architecture. He delights in hunting, but cares nothing for shooting; yet he is of a happy and cheerful disposition, and free from affectation. He is also a good, steady officer of Volunteers, and much liked by all who know him. Withal he is not yet four-and-thirty, he has been married nearly four years to the daughter of Lord Dorrington, and he has one son."

Vanity Fair, 1 October 1881

28
SPY (SIR LESLIE WARD) (1851-1922)
The Duke of Norfolk
'Our Little Duke'
Signed
Watercolour and bodycolour on tinted paper
12 x 7 inches
Provenance: Thomas Gibson Bowles;
The John Franks Collection
Illustrated: *Vanity Fair*, 1 October 1881, Statesmen no 374,
'Our Little Duke'

SPY (SIR LESLIE WARD) (1851-1922)
Sir John Bennett

The son of a watchmaker, Sir John Bennett (1814-1897) took over the business after his father's death. He promoted his company extensively in the media and it grew into a highly successful business, becoming a limited company in 1889. Bennett was a common councilman for Cheap ward, London from 1860 to 1888. In 1871 he was elected Sheriff of London and Middlesex and was knighted on 14 March 1872. He stood for parliament three times, in 1873, 1874 and 1886 but was unsuccessful on each occasion.

'Clocks'

"Sixty-eight years ago a son was born to an estimable citizen of Greenwich. Providence filled up the child with a certain set of brains, an unexaggerated collection of scruples, and a remarkable head of hair. Equipped with these gifts, John Bennett faced the world, and in due time rose to be a clockmaker. He advertised timepieces with such skill that he gradually became a light of the City, and was able to bestow his energies on popular education and other useful subjects. In the midst of these labours he found time to captivate the Fair, and thus (as he believes) he earned the jealousy of the Court of Aldermen. These envious persons have never allowed Sir John to become Lord Mayor; but he revenges himself by taking volumes of popular applause and by captivating the Fair more than ever."

Vanity Fair, 13 January 1883

29
Spy (Sir Leslie Ward) (1851-1922)
Sir John Bennett
'Clocks'
Signed
Watercolour and bodycolour with pencil
12 x 7 ½ inches
Illustrated: *Vanity Fair*, 13 January 1883, Men of the Day no 272, 'Clocks'

SPY (SIR LESLIE WARD) (1851-1922)
The Honourable Charles Spencer Bateman-Hanbury-Kincaid-Lennox

Charles Spencer Bateman-Hanbury-Kincaid-Lennox (1827-1912) was a Conservative politician who sat as MP for Herefordshire between 1852 and 1857, and for Leominster from 1858 to 1865. Known as Charles Bateman-Hanbury until 1862, he assumed, along with his wife, by Royal License the additional surnames of Kincaid-Lennox in accordance with his father-in-law's will.

'Charlie'

"The Hanburys having assumed the name of Bateman and been promoted to the peerage, Mr Charles Hanbury, being a younger son, after having been at Eton and gotten for himself a fellowship of All Souls College, was left to earn distinction for himself. So, after fourteen years, he changed his fellowship of All Souls for a fellowship in matrimony, and assumed the names of Kincaid-Lennox which were those originally borne by his wife. His friends however know him as 'Charlie'.

He is a man of five-and-fifty he stood for the county of Hereford, and, after a six months' contest, turned out the late Sir George Cornwall Lewis from the seat for that county. He next sat for Leominster, and was altogether for thirteen years in the House of Commons, where he became very popular, and whither he still proposes to return. He was also for ten years in the 2nd Life Guards; he is extremely well-known; he is much liked; and he walks nineteen stone."

Vanity Fair, 7 July 1883

30
SPY (SIR LESLIE WARD) (1851-1922)
The Honourable Charles Spencer
Bateman-Hanbury-Kincaid-Lennox
'Charlie'
Signed
Watercolour and bodycolour with pencil
12 ½ x 7 inches
Provenance: Thomas Gibson Bowles;
The John Franks Collection
Illustrated: *Vanity Fair*, 7 July 1883, Men of the Day no 288, 'Charlie'
Exhibited: 'Vanity Fair 1869-1914', Church Farm House Museum,
Hendon, September-December 1983

SPY (SIR LESLIE WARD) (1851-1922)
The Earl of Seafield

Ian Charles Ogilvy-Grant was a Conservative politician and the 27th Chief of Clan Grant. His portrait in *Vanity Fair* is titled 'Sheep' after the nickname given to him while he was serving in the First Regiment of Life Guards between 1869 and 1877. He sat in the House of Lords until his death at the age of 32, just a few months after he appeared in *Vanity Fair*. As he was unmarried and childless, the earldom passed to his uncle, James Ogilvy-Grant. The present portrait was produced by Leslie Ward in 1917 as a gift to Lady Nina Knowles, the daughter of Francis Ogilvy-Grant, the 10th Earl of Seafield.

'Sheep'

"The Ogilvies are a good and ancient Scottish family, who have long been important in their own country. One of them was made a Peer early in the seventeenth century, under the title of Findlater, and another of them soon became famous as a lawyer; so that in the first year of the eighteenth century they acquired the Earldom of Seafield.

The present and eighth Earl of Seafield is an excellent young man of two-and-thirty. The son of a most amiable and affectionate mother, he was sent to Eton, and at eighteen – being then Lord Reidhaven – went into the First Life Guards, the irreverent subalterns whereof endowed him with the nickname of 'Sheep.' He lived and soldiered in the regiment for eight years with credit and decency, and, having retired in 1877 from the career of arms, he succeeded in 1881 to his title, to his estates, and to a great affection for his native Scotland. In Scotland he lives for eight months of the year, and devotes himself to his local duties, to deerstalking, and to fishing. He is a sound Conservative, has done much earnest work for his Party, and although he has never yet made a speech in the House of Lords, he always may be relied upon for his vote. He is entirely without conceit or pretension; is simple, unaffected, honest, and altogether an excellent person."

Vanity Fair, 29 September 1883

31
Spy (Sir Leslie Ward) (1851-1922)
The Earl of Seafield
'Sheep'
Signed, inscribed 'Vanity Fair' and dated 'Sept. 29 1883'
Inscribed on reverse 'This picture belongs to Lady Nina Knowles, presented by the artist 'Spy' – Dec 1917'
Watercolour and bodycolour
13 ¾ x 7 ¾ inches
Illustrated: Similar to *Vanity Fair*, 29 September 1883,
Statesmen no 434, 'Sheep'

SPY (SIR LESLIE WARD) (1851-1922)
Mr Richard Quain, MD, FRS

As a house surgeon at University College Hospital, Sir Richard Quain (1816-1898) developed a reputation as one of London's leading physicians. From 1845 he was a leader writer for *The Lancet* and in 1846 was one of the founding members of the Pathological Society, becoming its president in 1869. He was assistant physician from 1848 to 1855, and physician from 1855 to 1875, at Brompton Hospital for Diseases of the Chest and was also consulting physician to the Royal Naval Hospital at Greenwich and the Royal Hospital for Consumption at Ventnor. From the 1850s, his reputation as a general physician on Harley Street earned him a number of high profile patients, including Benjamin Disraeli. In 1871 Quain was elected a fellow of the Royal Society and became Vice-President of the Royal College of Physicians in 1889. The following year, he was appointed Physician-Extraordinary to Queen Victoria.

'Lord Beaconsfield's Physician'

"Born seven-and-sixty years ago at Mallow, Dr. Quain was articled as pupil to an apothecary, and thus learned the properties of drugs – a knowledge which has been of much use to him in their administration, and has given him a belief in the power of physic. Coming later to London, he studied medicine at University College, and graduated at the London University, which has elected him a member of its Senate. He it is who enriched pathology with a new horror by discovering the true nature of fatty degeneration of the heart, and he holds a marked and foremost rank in the profession to which he belongs.

Dr. Quain is a man of no leisure. He is an untiring worker, and after seeing patients all days, edits a Dictionary of Medicine during most of the night. Yet he finds time every year for a certain amount of deerstalking, and thus prepares himself, by slaying in the Highlands, for a fresh course of healing in London. He is an amiable and agreeable man, full of good stories. He was Lord Beaconsfield's physician."

Vanity Fair, 15 December 1883

32
SPY (SIR LESLIE WARD) (1851-1922)
Mr Richard Quain, MD, FRS
'Lord Beaconsfield's Physician'
Signed
Inscribed 'Quain' on reverse
Watercolour and bodycolour
11 ½ x 6 ¾ inches
Illustrated: *Vanity Fair*, 15 December 1883, Men of the Day no 292, 'Lord Beaconsfield's Physician'

APE (CARLO PELLEGRINI) (1839-1889)
M. Paul Lessar

Paul Lessar (1851-1905) was a Russian Councillor and diplomat at the Russian Embassy in London between 1883 and 1901. In 1901, he left London to take up the post of Russian plenipotentiary in Peking. He died in 1905 from complications after an operation to amputate his foot.

'The Affghan Frontier'

"The appointment by the Russian Government of M. Paul Lessar as 'Diplomatic Attaché to the Governor of the Transcaspian,' and his employment as an Expert-Envoy to London in the matter of the Affghan Frontier, afford a striking example of the skill with which the Russian Cabinet selects its agents. M. Lessar is not by profession a Diplomatist, nor is he by race a Russian; for he was brought up as a civil engineer, and he comes of a Montenegrin family; yet to him has been committed the real direction of the most important and delicate act of that diplomacy by which Russia has obtained the consent of England to the extinction of Affghanistan, and to the permanent establishment of a Russian force within touch of England's tender spot in her Eastern Empire. To take a young foreign civil engineer and to make of him a Diplomatic Envoy on a matter of capital importance, merely because he thoroughly understood the matter and was a man of ability, would in England be accounted as impossible as absurd; but in Russia these affairs are directed neither by the intrigues of a Court nor by the traditions of a Foreign Office, but by the decisions of a trained conclave – the result of which is that the best man is taken, whatever he may be, and wherever he may be found. And M. Lessar is undoubtedly admirably suited for the part he has had given to him to play.

Born four-and-thirty years ago, M. Lessar was educated at the école des ingénieurs in St. Petersburg. Being found to have brains, courage, and energy, he was allowed to accompany General Skobeleff into Asia in order to survey for railways, and in 1880 was attached to General Komaroff, as an expert in surveying and exploration, to work in the Turcoman country between the Caspian and Affghanistan. Established at the advanced station of Askabad, M. Lessar made constant excursions, attended only by a few converted Turcoman brigands; and in November, 1881, he adventured himself through and beyond Sarakhs, across the Affghan frontier, and to within a few miles of Herat, mapping as he went, and remarking, with pleasure, of the Tekke Turcomans who sought to hinder him, that 'these sons of the desert are not masters of the art of lying.' So extended and constant were his journeys, that in the course of two years he rode a distance of nearly six thousand miles, having upon occasions ridden no less than ninety-seven miles in the day upon a single horse; and there is probably no living man who knows so well as he the whole ground of the Russo-Persian and Russo-Affghan frontier, or who is so well able to put his finger upon the points thereof that are politically doubtful or militarily important.

Personally M. Lessar is silent and self-contained, yet amiable and courteous, a man of many labours, of much knowledge, of a great, quiet determination, and of a temper which makes him ready to sacrifice not merely ease and comfort, but even life itself to the acquisition of greater powers to deal with his work. He speaks English a little, and French very well. He is a dangerous antagonist."

Vanity Fair, 19 September 1885

33
Ape (Carlo Pellegrini) (1839-1889)
M. Paul Lessar
'The Affghan Frontier'
Signed
Inscribed 'Lessar (M Paul) "The Afghan Frontier"' on reverse
Watercolour with pencil
12 x 7 inches
Provenance: Thomas Gibson Bowles;
The John Franks Collection
Illustrated: *Vanity Fair*, 19 September 1885, Men of the Day 341,
'The Affghan Frontier'

34
Spy (Sir Leslie Ward) (1851-1922)
Sir James Taylor Ingham, MA, Knight
'Bow Street'
Signed
Watercolour with bodycolour and pencil
16 ¼ x 10 ¾ inches
Provenance: The Dibben Family, Nash Priory and 4 Smith Square,
London SW1
Illustrated: *Vanity Fair*, 20 February 1886, Men of the Day no 353,
'Bow Street'
Literature: Morris L Cohen, *The Bench and Bar, Great Legal
Caricatures from 'Vanity Fair' by Spy*, New Haven, CT: Hugh Lauter
Levin Associates, 1997, page 32

SPY (SIR LESLIE WARD) (1851-1922)
Sir James Taylor Ingham, MA, Knight

Yorkshire-born James Taylor Ingham (1805-1890) was called to
the bar at the Inner Temple, and initially joined the Northern
Circuit, becoming a magistrate in London in 1849. He was made
Chief Magistrate of London in 1876, sitting at Bow Street. Later
that year, he was knighted at Osborne House.

'Bow Street'

*"The Chief Magistrate at Bow Street was born in the year in
which the reign of King George the Third was glorified by the
Battle of Trafalgar; consequently his early career is a matter of
ancient history.*

*In the reign of King George the Fourth he was admitted as a
student at the Inner Temple; and in the reign of King William the
Fourth he graduated as an M.A. at Trinity College, Cambridge, and
was called to the Bar. He joined the Northern Circuit and practised
at the West Riding Sessions, most naturally, since his father
– Mr. Joshua Ingham, late of Blake Hall and Knowle House – was
a Yorkshire gentleman; but his prowess as an advocate has faded
out of living memory.*

*Two years before Queen Victoria came to the Throne, he married a
Miss Penrose, from Ireland; and in 1849 he was appointed one of
the Magistrates of the Thames Police Court. In 1876 he succeeded
the late Sir Thomas Henry as the Chief of the twenty-three
Metropolitan Police Magistrates, which position he still efficiently
occupies, and was honoured with a Knighthood in return for his
very protracted services.*

*He is a Justice of the Peace for the West Riding of Yorkshire, for
Middlesex, and for Berkshire; he understands his business perfectly
well, although his eighty-first birthday is over and gone; and there
appears to be plenty of life in him yet.*

*Sir James Ingham is an ornament to the Magisterial Bench.
His vast experience renders him extremely reliable in all that he
does. He is an authority on International Law; wherefore cases
involving points of difficulty under the various Extradition Treaties
are always taken to Bow Street. His name is connected with all the
Police Court causes-célèbres which have arisen during the last
dozen years, from the trials of the Dynamitists for treason-felony
down to the investigation of the locus standi of so-called
proprietary gambling clubs. He displays a nose betokening much
shrewd sense. His manner is courteous, with a quietly sarcastic
tinge which is often very effective; yet he is a dignified Magistrate,
never descending to that buffoonery which comes so ill from the
Bench, and his Court is therefore always well ordered. He is a rival
to Vice-Chancellor Bacon in his green and vigorous old age.
He is a gentleman, and he draws a salary of £1800 a-year."*

Vanity Fair, 20 February 1886

SPY (SIR LESLIE WARD) (1851-1922)
Mr George Granville Leveson-Gower

The nephew of the Foreign Secretary Earl Granville, Sir George Granville Leveson-Gower (1858-1951) first entered into politics as Private Secretary to William Gladstone in 1880, a position he held throughout Gladstone's second government. From 1885 to 1886 he was Liberal MP for North-West Staffordshire. After losing his seat in 1886, he was returned as MP for Stoke-on-Trent in 1890 and held the seat until 1895. He wrote regularly for the periodicals and in 1899 became european editor of the *North American Review*.

'My Dear George'

"In the ill-fated Parliament which recently expired, a sturdy and rather hearty-looking young man, but good-humoured withal, was among the most regular of all the Members attending the House of Commons. He came early and stayed late. In the small hours of the morning, after a long and wearisome sitting, he sometimes took furtive naps on the Treasury Bench; but as a rule he was brisk and watchful, and cheerfully aided the chief Liberal Whips in their duties. Moreover he read out at question-time, with suitable emphasis, the replies to such Parliamentary conundrums as were addressed to the Office of Works, and altogether he gave on-lookers the impression that he dearly loved the House of Commons and the labours of a Junior Lord of the Treasury. But Mr. George Leveson-Gower, for such was the name of this plodding Junior Lord, has ceased to be a Member of Parliament, and the Treasury Bench knows him no more. Probably, however, his exile is only temporary, for a nephew of Lord Granville and a former private secretary to Mr. Gladstone, does not, as a rule, sink below the horizon never to be heard of again. His late constituency, North-West Staffordshire, rejected him at the General Election, but no doubt Mr. Leveson-Gower – apostrophised by Mr. Gladstone as 'My dear George' has been more than compensated for his defeat by receiving an autograph letter from his friend and patron denouncing the 'blackguardism and baseness' of William Pitt. Hitherto Mr. Leveson-Gower has not given much promise of statesmanship, but as he is yet on the sunny-side of thirty his friends have not abandoned the hope that he may some day rise to the dignity of an Under-Secretary. Failing that, the inevitable Commissionership with which Mr. Gladstone's private secretaries are rewarded will probably be his lot. He is a kind-hearted, modest, unobtrusive youth, and is not deficient in common sense of the solid type. He has no enemies, because he is of no consequence."

Vanity Fair, 14 August 1886

35
SPY (SIR LESLIE WARD) (1851-1922)
Mr George Granville Leveson-Gower
'My Dear George'
Signed
Watercolour with bodycolour and pencil
11 ½ x 7 inches
Illustrated: *Vanity Fair*, 14 August 1886, Men of the Day no 363,
'My Dear George'

SPY (SIR LESLIE WARD) (1851-1922)
Mr Charles Beilby Stuart-Wortley, MP

Trained as a QC, Charles Stuart-Wortley (1851-1926) came to the bar at Inner Temple in 1876. In 1880, he became the first Conservative to elected as an MP for Sheffield. He was named under-secretary for the Home Office in 1885 and again from 1886 to 1892. In 1917, he was created Baron Stuart of Wortley.

'Sheffield'

"Born five-and-thirty years ago into the old and honourable Yorkshire family of which the Earl of Wharncliffe is the head, Mr. Charles Beilby Stuart-Wortley is a younger son of the late Right Honourable James Stuart-Wortley, Q.C. On his mother's side he is connected with the Wenlocks of Salop. After a course of Rugby and Balliol he went to the Bar, and, by dint of industriously plodding for some years on the North-Eastern Circuit, he gained that insight into the ways of malefactors which has since proved useful to him in another sphere of public service. At the bidding of a still small voice he contrived to make his way into Parliament, and since 1880 he has sat without interruption for Sheffield, first as one of the Members of the undivided borough, and afterwards for the Hallam Division. Last year, when the Tories floated into office on the wreckage of Mr. Childers's Budget, Mr. Stuart-Wortley was sent to the Home Office as Under-Secretary, and for some months he dutifully sat at the feet of Gamaliel, personified by Sir Richard Cross. By the recent Unionist victory, he returns to his old position. There is no reason why he should not get on. He has sufficient confidence in himself; he is not unacquainted with law; he is a hard worker and 'thorough' in everything he undertakes; and he is altogether devoid of that dangerous gift of brilliancy which is sometimes resented by a man's official superiors. Without being a good speaker, he knows how to make a clear statement, and his natural caution prevents him from discussing subjects which he does not understand. Therefore he is esteemed, and justly so, a safe man, and the soundness of his Toryism has never been questioned. By his feats in pigeon-shooting and his marriage with a daughter of Sir J. E. Millais, Mr. Stuart-Wortley's name has come to be faintly known and echoed outside the ring of Parliament and the High Court of Justice. He has not improved his appearance by shaving off his beard."

Vanity Fair, 11 September 1886

36
Spy (Sir Leslie Ward) (1851-1922)
Mr Charles Beilby Stuart-Wortley, MP
'Sheffield'
Pencil sketch of heads and inscribed 'C B Stuart-Wortley' on reverse
Watercolour with bodycolour and pencil on tinted paper
13 x 7 inches
Illustrated: Preliminary Drawing for *Vanity Fair*, 11 September 1886, Statesmen no 498, 'Sheffield'

APE (CARLO PELLEGRINI) (1839-1889)
Lord Egerton of Tatton

The only son of the 1st Baron Egerton, Wilbraham Egerton (1832-1909) was a Justice of the Peace for Cheshire and a captain in the Earl of Chester's Yeomanry Cavalry before becoming Conservative MP for North Cheshire in 1858. In 1868 the seat was reorganised and he became MP for Mid Cheshire until 1883, when he succeeded his father's title and moved to the House of Lords. He became the 1st Earl Egerton in 1897.

'Tatton'

"The Egertons appear to have first been de Malpas's and of Norman origin, but five hundred years ago they got the manor of Egerton, took its name as their own. Four hundred years ago, Ralph Egerton left a natural son who became Lord Chancellor as Viscount Brackley, and from whom sprang the families of the Earls of Bridgewater. The third son of the second Earl of Bridgewater was Thomas Egerton of Tatton; and Tatton descended to his grandson, when, on the male line failing, it passed to his granddaughter, Esther Egerton, whose husband took her maiden name. Their daughter married in the last century one of the Sykes's of Sledmere, and the history of the race is thenceforth a hash of Egertons, Tattons, and Sykes's. The family however was rich, respectable, and respected, and in 1859 William Tatton Egerton was elevated to the Peerage as the first Baron Egerton of Tatton. He married a daughter of the second Lord Ely, who long was famous as one of the London great ladies, cited for her wit, her haughtiness, her assurance, and her parties, and who is still a living tradition in London Society as the now lamented 'Tattie.'

The present, and second, Lord Egerton is the son of the great lady, was born four-and-fifty years ago, was sent, as became him, to Eton and to Oxford, and in 1858, when he was six-and-twenty, was elected to Parliament for Mid-Cheshire, which he represented till in 1883 he succeeded his father in the title and the estates. The inheritance was a rich one, for it comprised much land in Cheshire and Lancashire, including a good deal in, and close to, Manchester, which is of great value. Lord Egerton therefore is a wealthy man; he is also an honourable and a kindly man, a good landlord, and a sound Tory. Throughout Cheshire and a good part of Lancashire the name of Egerton has long been one to swear by, and the present Peer has added to its popularity and its power by his personal rectitude and his industry in all the unpaid works of public service. He is not an orator, but he is an Ecclesiastical Commissioner, and he is never found wanting when a man of position is looked for in the North to take a part in any public undertaking. He is a gentleman."

Vanity Fair, 27 November 1886

37
APE (CARLO PELLEGRINI) (1839-1889)
Lord Egerton of Tatton
'Tatton'
Signed
Watercolour
12 x 7 inches
Provenance: Thomas Gibson Bowles; Stanley Jackson;
The John Franks Collection
Illustrated: *Vanity Fair*, 27 November 1886, Statesmen no 506,
'Tatton'

Spy (Sir Leslie Ward) (1851-1922)
Mr Frank Lockwood, QC, MP

Frank Lockwood (1846-1897) was a famous lawyer and Liberal MP for York in the period 1885-97. Having been called to the bar in 1872, he went on to become Solicitor-General in Lord Rosebery's ministry for the year 1894-95, and was knighted at the same time. A talented amateur artist, he published *The Frank Lockwood Sketch Book* in 1898.

'York'

"Great grandson of a respectable stonemason who afterwards became Mayor of Doncaster, he was rough-hewn in the same Yorkshire town about one-and-forty years ago, and his ends were shaped at the Manchester Grammar School, and Caius College, Cambridge. Leaving the latter seat of learning with rather less knowledge than when he went up, he migrated to Lincoln's Inn, and in due course was added to the overstocked profession of the Bar, in which however, by reason of ready wit, a bluff and wholesome presence, a rich voice, a good deal of law, and some self-confidence, he managed to make headway. Finding his talents wasted at the Chancery Bar, where on one occasion he nearly caused the late Lord Romilly to have a fit, he laid himself out for advocacy. He defended the malefactor affectionately known to juvenile students of criminal literature as 'Charley Peace'; he tickled North Country juries with his jokes; he cross-examined with shrewdness and effect; until at length without him no case of libel, breach of promise, or horse-coping was complete. After ten years as a junior – during which period of probation he executed the best and most beneficial contract of his career by marrying a daughter of the house of Salis-Schwabe - he 'took silk.' Such an early venture would have been risky for a man less well provided for; but with Mr. Lockwood it was a complete success. And he is now one of the leaders of the Bar, and one of the best-liked men in England.

Turning his eyes Parliament-wards, he contrived to get defeated at Lynn; but he now sits for York as one of that self-denying flock of politicians whose Mecca is Mid-Lothian. He can make a capital electioneering speech; as an expert handler of witnesses he is unsurpassed; and he is the idol of the Junior Bar, for whose edification he covers reams of paper with pen-and-ink sketches. He never makes the mistake of sending a Judge a caricature of himself, but always that of a learned brother. He rides better than he shoots, and talks much better than he rides; but he is a sportsman to the backbone, and the burning of his grouse moor near Scarborough the other day is a misfortune which has gained for him the sympathy of all his friends. He labours under the suspicion of having once been a Tory, but he has taken more pains to deny the impeachment than its gravity perhaps warrants. He is a thoroughly good all-round man."

Vanity Fair, 20 August 1887

38
SPY (SIR LESLIE WARD) (1851-1922)
Mr Frank Lockwood, QC, MP
'York'
Signed
Watercolour and pencil on tinted paper
7 ½ x 12 inches
Illustrated: *Vanity Fair*, 20 August 1887, Statesmen no 526, 'York'
Literature: Morris L Cohen, *The Bench and Bar, Great Legal Caricatures from 'Vanity Fair' by Spy*, New Haven, CT: Hugh Lauter Levin Associates, 1997, page 38

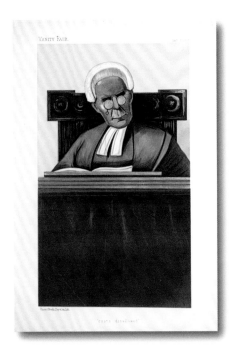

39
SPY (SIR LESLIE WARD) (1851-1922)
The Hon. Sir Edward Ebenezer Kay
'Costs Disallowed'
Signed and dated 1888
Ink
4 ½ x 4 inches
Illustrated: Preliminary Drawing for *Vanity Fair*, 7 January 1888,
Judges no 20, 'Costs Disallowed'
Illustrated: *Vanity Fair*, 20 August 1887, Statesmen no 526, 'York'
Literature: Morris L Cohen, **The Bench and Bar, Great Legal**
Caricatures from 'Vanity Fair' by Spy, New Haven, CT: Hugh Lauter
Levin Associates, 1997, page 40

SPY (SIR LESLIE WARD) (1851-1922)
The Hon. Sir Edward Ebenezer Kay

Sir Edward Ebenezer Kay (1822-1897) was a high court judge,
appointed justice of the High Court, Chancery Division in March
1881 and knighted in May of the same year. In November 1890
he succeeded Sir Henry Cotton as Lord Justice of Appeal.

'Costs Disallowed'

*"Born to Robert Kay, Esq., of Rochdale, Lancashire, six-and-sixty
years go, Sir Edward Ebenezer Kay has since played successively
the parts of Cambridge undergraduate, son-in-law of the late
Master of Jesus, law reporter, Queen's Counsel, Chairman of
Quarter Sessions, Judge of the High Court, and, above all, protector
of the widowed and fatherless. He does not come of a public school,
but he has missed no opportunity of assimilating equity and (since
he has been a Judge) of cutting down legal costs in all directions.
His unjudicial career lasted until 1881, when, after having
practised as a 'special' before the House of Lords for three years, he
was raised to the Bench (which had just been vacated by
Vice-Chancellor Malins) by Lord Selborne, who has since had no
reason to regret the appointment.*

*Mr. Justice Kay is pre-eminently a Judge with a special mission.
He is very fond of disallowing costs on the slightest provocation.
It is always the duty of his Court 'to protect this fund,' when in
administration or trust cases, costs are asked 'out of the estate.'
He often threatens 'to take vigorous measures' to protect such funds,
and no one doubts his will or his power to do so. Sometimes he
goes too far in this 'full determination' of his; then the Court of
Appeal sets him right, and the law costs of that case are worse than
the first. Lawyers do not like Mr. Justice Kay, and they say nasty
things about his not having discovered his mission until he left the
Bar for the Bench; but infants and widows owe him a debt of
gratitude, and some of them are grateful to him, which is the surest
possible sign that he has done very much for them. Beyond this
Mr. Justice Kay differs from the average Judge only in his personal
appearance, in his knowledge of Equity, and in his manners. He is
gifted with a strong sense of his own importance, and strives, with
considerable success, to look as good a Judge as he is. He is more
than sufficiently dignified to excite extreme respect for that majesty
of the Law which he never misses the smallest chance of vindicating
in season and out of season. His knowledge of Equity is abstruse,
and he seems to remember all the details of all the cases reported
in 'Kay's Reports' and 'Kay and Johnson's Reports,' by which he
long ago immortalised the name of Kay. But his manners are
imperfect. He has often been rude to counsel; he delights to say
nasty things of and to solicitors; and he frightens witnesses. His
voice grates, and his manner repels. He has a long upper lip which
he is able to wreathe with an unpleasant curl. He is a martinet.
He is a godsend to the Incorporated Law Society, which keeps a list
of his more robust utterances ever ready to hurl at the heads of
straying sheep of its rather mixed flock, But he is a good and strong
Judge, who is able to get through a cause-list with equal celerity
and certainty."*

Vanity Fair, 7 January 1888

Leslie Ward.
1888.

'Financial News'

AJM (Arthur H Marks) (active 1889)
Harry Marks

Born in London, Harry Marks (1855-1916) moved to the United States at the age of sixteen, where he would remain until 1883. He began his journalistic career in Texas, before moving to New York. In 1883, he returned to London and established himself as the chief proprietor and editor of the *Financial and Mining News*, London's first financial daily, predating the *Financial Times* by 4 years. The paper became extremely popular, in a sector that had developed a dull reputation. It held a strong line in investigative journalism, exposing a vein of corruption in the Metropolitan Board of Works in 1888. Marks entered politics in 1889 as a member of the first London county council, but failed to become MP for Bethnal Green in 1892. In 1895 he gained a narrow victory at St George-in-the-East, a seat he held until 1900.

'Financial News'

"His father, the Rev. Professor Marks, Dean of University College, sent him to College in Belgium, after which ten years' residence in the United States taught Harry Marks the way to make a big newspaper property in London in half that time. His Financial News is but a little more than five years old, and he is its chief proprietor and editor.

To pilot such a paper through all the difficulties which encumber the path of a new journal, to fight and win eighteen libel suits in five years, would require all the time and all the energy of any ordinary man. But Harry Marks, not being an ordinary man, found that one paper was not enough for him. So two years ago he started the Evening Post. Even this did not satisfy his greed for work and power, and accordingly, three months ago, he absorbed it into the Evening News, making of the two an enterprising Unionist evening journal.

From newspapers to politics being but a step, he was returned at the top of his poll to that ill-begotten County Council which he had helped to call into being. He is a Unionist, and North-East Bethnal Green has adopted him as its candidate for Parliament. He is married and his wife is training a young editor to succeed him. He is fond of horses, and owns a promising colt, which lately began to carry his colours at Newmarket. He has a fine picture gallery, wears tight boots, suffers from gout, and is fond of music. He cannot sing, though he sometimes tries to do so."

Vanity Fair, 8 June 1889

40
AJM (Arthur H Marks) (active 1889)
Harry Marks
'Financial News'
Signed
Watercolour and bodycolour
11 ½ x 7 inches
Illustrated: *Vanity Fair*, 8 June 1889, Men of the Day no 428,
'Financial News'

LIB (LIBORIO PROSPERI) (1854-1928)
Mr Geo Egerton

At the time of his portrait in *Vanity Fair*, George Mark Leycester Egerton (1837-1898) was serving as the official handicapper for the Jockey Club. Founded in 1750 (though some claim as early as the 1710s), the Jockey Club was a high societal meeting place for those passionate about horseracing. Initially meetings were held in London at the Star and Garter in Pall Mall and also in St James' Street and Hyde Park. In 1752, the Jockey Club leased a plot of land in Newmarket where a coffee house was constructed in the High Street as a meeting place. They soon purchased the freehold and the meeting place became known as the Jockey Club Rooms, which still exists today. The role of the handicapper was to decide on what handicap weights were assigned to which horses in an attempt to equalise the competitive field.

'Our Handicapper'

"Three years ago he was made Official Handicapper to the Jockey Club, which absolute body has since had no reason to regret his appointment; but long before that he was an acknowledged authority on the merits of horses, as he often showed by amateur handicapping in a small way. Every inch of his six feet is an inch of a soldier, though he is now rounder than he was when he marched with the Rifle Brigade before the grey began to show upon him; yet his manners are mild enough to conceal the firmness of his unyielding disposition from those who know him only on the surface. He is full of racing lore, and could revise the proofs of 'Ruff' without reference; for he is so devoted, both by profession and inclination, to the Turf and to performances thereon that it is very hard for the most knowing sportsman to get round him, although he always looks at things through a single eye-glass, and therefore, presumably, has a blind side. He is so straight that it would be absurd to say that his work gives general satisfaction to racing men, unless it be assumed that most racing men are straight; and when – as is the case a few men on the Turf are found to object to the way in which he applies his weights to their horses, their objections to his methods are but a tribute to his merits. He lives near Doncaster, and acquits himself excellently well in a very thankless office. He is a good, honest fellow."

Vanity Fair, 24 August 1889

41
LIB (LIBORIO PROSPERI) (1854-1928)
Mr Geo Egerton
'Our Handicapper'
Signed, inscribed with title and dated 1886
Watercolour and pencil with bodycolour
14 ½ x 9 ½ inches
Provenance: Thomas Gibson Bowles; The John Franks Collection
Illustrated: Similar to *Vanity Fair*, 24 August 1889, Men of the Day no 437, 'Official Handicapper to the Jockey Club'
Exhibited: 'In Vanity Fair', Stanford University, San Francisco, September-November 1980; 'Vanity Fair 1869-1914', Church Farm House Museum, Hendon, September-December 1983

Mr. Geo: Egerton
our Handicapper.
1886.

'The Sheffield Daily Telegraph'

Sir William Christopher Leng

In 1864 Sir William Christopher Leng (1825-1902), who had begun his journalistic career contributing to the *Hull Free Press* and *Dundee Advertister*, joined Frederick Clifford (1828-1904) in purchasing the *Sheffield Daily Telegraph*. He became its managing editor and rapidly turned the paper into a great Conservative power in the north of England. Leng expanded his publishing business to include a *Weekly Telegraph*, a *Sunday Telegraph*, and the *Evening Telegraph* and *Star*. He also remained active as a journalist, reporting for the *Daily Telegraph* on his travels in Europe. He was also politically active, serving as vice-chairman and chairman of the Sheffield Conservative and Constitutional Association. On the recommendation of Lord Salisbury, who referred to the *Sheffield Daily Telegraph* as that 'clever organ of Jingoism', Leng was knighted in the Jubilee honours of 1887.

'The Sheffield Daily Telegraph'

"Born five-and-sixty years ago at Hull, he was brought up in the chemists trade, from which wholesome occupation he was diverted by his greed for work into the paths of journalistic enterprise. In 1859 he wrote for The Dundee Advertiser. In 1890 he is the editor and managing proprietor of The Sheffield Daily Telegraph. He owes a good deal to one named William Broadhead, for it was by his dogged and aggressive war with Broadheadism that he earned for himself the little niche which he now occupies. Having successfully suppressed this form of trade tyranny, and having brought about a Royal Commission of Inquiry into Trades' Union Outrages in Sheffield, he was obliged to take his own portrait and six hundred guineas from the good and grateful Yorkshire folk; and, continuing to prosper, he was three years ago improved into an excellent but rather pompous Jubilee Knight.

Despite the mental and physical activity which, combined with British obstinacy, has made him what he is, Sir William is a very absent-minded man. He is therefore a complete fortune to spectacle-makers and to purveyors of umbrellas; for while he has unavailingly bought spectacles by the gross, he very constantly forgets to bring either his own or any other person's umbrella home with him: which is quite absurd. He is an aggressive, roundly abusive, scornful denunciator of his foes, who gives less time to the ransacking of Hansard than he spares space for invective; for it is his chief article of belief that Conservatism prospers by aggression. He found Sheffield a hot-bed of Radicalism and he converted it, and became a Town Trustee and a member of the Chamber of Commerce. He is equally fond of a good story and of long Partagas, which he smokes all day, and smoking which he falls asleep.

It is his boast that he earned his breakfast before he was eleven years old; yet he is a conceited man, for he is so particular about the company which he keeps that he is said to have declined to seek Parliamentary honours."

Vanity Fair, 8 March 1890

42
Spy (Sir Leslie Ward) (1851-1922)
Sir William Christopher Leng
'The Sheffield Daily Telegraph'
Signed
Watercolour with bodycolour and pencil on tinted paper
12 x 6 ¾ inches
Illustrated: *Vanity Fair*, 8 March 1890, Men of the Day no 463,
'The Sheffield Daily Telegraph'

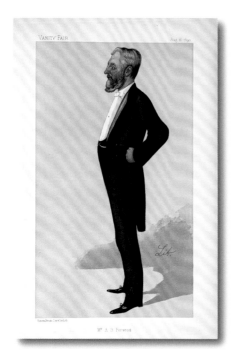

LIB (LIBORIO PROSPERI) (1854-1928)
Mr Arthur Bower Forwood, MP

As a politician and public servant, Sir Arthur Forwood (1836-1898) did a great deal to raise the standing of the city of Liverpool in Britain following the industrial revolution. He proved himself a skilled businessman in the shipping industry before joining Liverpool's municipal council in 1871. He served as a councillor for 27 years and was Mayor of Liverpool from 1878 to 1879. In 1885 he became Conservative MP for Ormskirk, a seat he held until his death. In 1886, Lord Salisbury appointed him as Parliamentary and Financial Secretary to the Admiralty, thus becoming the first shipowner to become an Admiralty minister.

'Mr A B Forwood'

"He was born into the family of Forwood, which for several generations has stood high among the shipowners of Liverpool, four-and-fifty years ago; and, though early initiated into the mysteries of charter-parties and of the export trade, he showed so great an aptitude for municipal affairs that his fellow-citizens marked his activity in the Corporation by creating him their Mayor at the age of forty-two. Then, pining to achieve something more than local renown, he proved himself so good and so discreet a Tory organiser that his opponents, less cynically than respectfully, dubbed him 'The Young Napoleon'; which title he did what in him lay to merit by contriving to return Mr. Whitley to the House of Commons in opposition to the late Lord Ramsay. Although thus able to procure seats for others, this Joseph Chamberlain of Liverpool remained seatless; and even suffered the humiliation of being beaten by good Mr. Samuel Smith. But he bided his time until 1885, when his patience was rewarded by the Ormskirk Division of Lancashire. And since it was meet that one who had done such service to his Party should receive prompt reward, he was presently made Secretary to the Admiralty – because he knew something of the Mercantile Marine.

By sticking closely to his desk, and by never going to sea, he has acquired a reputation for solidity and business aptitude, which is confirmed by a suitable heaviness of manner. He is an industrious official, who still finds time to cast a master's eye over the wealthy firm of which he is the head; and though to the casual observer he conveys the idea that he is highly impressed with the importance of Mr. Arthur Bower Forwood, this is rather the result of native awkwardness than any outward sign of vanity.

He invented the system of single-Member constituencies, and he has a brother who is a civic luminary and a Knight Bachelor. He helps to direct public Companies and he is a member of many Clubs. He is more practical than polished in his Manners."

Vanity Fair, 16 August 1890

43
LIB (LIBORIO PROSPERI) (1854-1928)
Mr Arthur Bower Forwood, MP
'Mr A B Forwood'
Signed
Inscribed with title on reverse
Watercolour and bodycolour on tinted paper
14 x 8 inches
Provenance: The John Franks Collection
Illustrated: *Vanity Fair*, 16 August 1890, Statesmen no 572,
'Mr A B Forwood'
Exhibited: 'Vanity Fair 1869-1914', Church Farm House Museum,
Hendon, September-December 1983

SPY (SIR LESLIE WARD) (1851-1922)
Mr Reuben David Sassoon

Rueben David Sassoon (1835-1905) was a prominent Jewish businessman and member of the vastly wealthy Sassoon family. His father, David Sassoon, as a trader in China and Treasurer to Baghdad from 1817 to 1829, had monopolised the Sino-Indian Opium trade in the nineteenth-century. Reuben Sassoon worked as a director for his father's company, David Sassoon & Co. and was on the Board of Directors of the China Steamship and Labuan Coal Company.

'Mr Reuben Sassoon'

"The third son of the late David Sassoon of Bombay, and one of a race of lucky Indian merchants, he went to China in his early youth; and, having made a fortune in business, he now spends his money royally. He is fond of the Play; and, being also fond of Sport, he has for some years had a few horses in Mr. Leopold de Rothschild's stable; Theodore, by Sir Bevys, being the best and most profitable that he has owned. He is a friend of the Prince of Wales, though he has not been with him at Homburg this season; and, having no enemies, he is popular in Society. He is full of charity, yet he is quite an unostentatious man.

He entertained the Shah."

Vanity Fair, 20 September 1890

44
SPY (SIR LESLIE WARD) (1851-1922)
Mr Reuben David Sassoon
'Mr Reuben Sassoon'
Signed
Watercolour and bodycolour on tinted paper
13 ½ x 10 inches
Illustrated: *Vanity Fair*, 20 September 1890, Men of the Day no 482, 'Mr Reuben Sassoon'

SPY (SIR LESLIE WARD) (1851-1922)
George Frederic Watts (1817-1904)

George Frederic Watts (1817-1904) was a painter and sculptor, who at the time of his appearance in *Vanity Fair*, had become the most revered figure in British art and one of the most famous artists in the world. He was one of the first artists to hold the Order of Merit, when it was instituted in 1902. Inspired by the example of the Renaissance masters, he attempted to revive the tradition of history painting by producing ambitious allegories that promoted a moral message, stating that 'I paint ideas, not things'. The allusive, often expressive results reveal an association with the Continental Symbolist movement. In addition, he was a distinctive and penetrating portraitist, and an occasional, but invariably impressive sculptor.

'He Paints Portraits & Ideas'

"He was born one-and-seventy years ago, so that his childhood and youth are matter of ancient history. But he must have begun to develop the Art that is in him with his first penny paint-box, for at the unripe age of seventeen he achieved exhibition at the Royal Academy. At twenty he had been guilty of several portraits and a scene from Boccaccio. A couple of years later he was bold enough to illustrate 'Cymbeline'; and immediately afterwards, by a representation of Caractacus led in triumph through the streets of Rome, he won a prize of £300. His success sent him to Italy, where his imagination was stimulated; and the Commissioners began to buy his work. He tossed off such trifles as 'Paolo and Francesca,' 'Orlando Pursuing the Fata Morgana,' 'Life's Illusions,' and other such scintillations of his brain in rapid succession; he evolved one of the frescoes in the Poets' Hall at West-minster, in which St. George is shown vanquishing the Dragon; and having done much other good work, he was elected a Royal Academician three-and-twenty years ago.

He paints portraits and ideas so well that, although he has not always attained complete success, he is yet unsurpassed as a powerful and original artist; while he has done work – of which his 'Hope' is a type – that is quite unequalled. He has painted a gallery full of portraits for his own house; which he is believed, and hoped, to have bequeathed to the Nation. He is always ready to encourage young artists; to whom he constantly preaches the conscientious study of Nature, knowing that from her he learned all that he knows of Art.

He is a cultivated man and a friend of Sir Frederick Leighton; yet he lives very plainly. He once refused a Baronetcy."

Vanity Fair, 19 December 1891

45
SPY (SIR LESLIE WARD) (1851-1922)
Mr George Frederic Watts, RA, DCL, LLD
'He Paints Portraits & Ideas'
Signed
Watercolour with pencil and bodycolour on tinted paper
12 ½ x 6 ¾ inches
Illustrated: *Vanity Fair*, 19 December 1891, Men of the Day no 526, 'He Paints Portraits & Ideas'
Exhibited: 'The Heatherley School of Fine Art, 150th Anniversary Exhibition', Mall Galleries, February-March 1996, no 81

SPY (SIR LESLIE WARD) (1851-1922)
Mr Edward Linley Sambourne

Linley Sambourne (1844-1910) was best known as a cartoonist and writer for *Punch*, where he would succeed Sir John Tenniel as chief political cartoonist in 1901. Educated at City of London School and Chester Training College School, Linley Sambourne initially apprenticed as a draughtsman to a firm of marine engineers in Greenwich. Though he had had only a short period of formal artistic training, his sketches caught the eye of the editor of *Punch*, Mark Lemon, and in 1867 he began drawing for the periodical. Four years later he joined the staff full-time, and became known for producing decorative initial letters to *Punch*'s 'The Essence of Parliament'. He gradually expanded these images, usurping the importance of Shirley Brooks' text and so providing a second political cartoon. In 1878, he was appointed 'cartoon junior', while, from the 1890s, he understudied Tenniel as political cartoonist, finally replacing him on his retirement in 1901. In addition to his work for *Punch*, Sambourne contributed to a few other magazines and illustrated books, including *The Water Babies* (1885) and *Three Tales of Hans Andersen* (published posthumously in 1910). He exhibited at the Royal Academy between 1885 and 1910, and his only solo show, at the Fine Art Society in 1893, was a sell-out success.

'Sammy'

"Historically he dates from 1815; but his cadly years having been passed in the obscurity of the nursery, the City of London School, Chester College, and an engineer's workshop, his career really and for all practical purposes began some four-and-twenty years ago. He was then devoting such time as he could spare from the more serious business of caricaturing other people to the art of engineering, under the roofs of John Penn and Son at Greenwich; when a good angel took one of his untaught sketches into the hands of Mark Lemon, who thereupon put a presentment of John Bright tilting at a quintain into Punch. Since then his countless original, humorous, and precisely detailed drawings for that paper have made his pencil well known to all the world. He has illustrated 'The Water Babies,' 'Hans Andersen's Fairy Tales,' and a shelf-full of other books; and he has designed a diploma for an International Exhibition, and has exhibited it at the Royal Academy. But he has not designed any of our beautiful coins.

Having been apprenticed to a maker of steam engines, he is naturally full of pictorial cranks and eccentric imaginings; yet he never wastes a line. He makes much and artistically unorthodox use of photographs, because his journalistic duties will not allow him time to draw from life; yet he is quite an artist. He has a keen eye for small detail, and for preciseness his work is unrivalled; but it is not therefore robbed of general effect. He never took lessons in drawing, yet he is a very accurate draughtsman, who always clothes his figures naturally. He can fill a page so full of humorous eccentricity that a moderately dull person may look at it for half an hour before he may appreciate all that is there.

He is a cheerful fellow, with nothing of the fop about him. He is unartistic to look at; he cares nothing for fashion; he is fond of riding; and he is more like a countryman than an artist. But he is not altogether what he seems, and there is often a twinkle in his eye."

Vanity Fair, 16 January 1892

46
SPY (SIR LESLIE WARD) (1851-1922)
Mr Edward Linley Sambourne
'Sammy'
Signed
Inscribed with title and dated 'Nov 1891' below mount
Watercolour with bodycolour
12 ½ x 9 inches
Illustrated: *Vanity Fair*, 16 January 1892, Men of the Day no 528, 'Sammy'

47
Spy (Sir Leslie Ward) (1851-1922)
The Right Honourable Sir Charles Synge
Christopher Bowen, PC, DCL, LLD, FRS
'Judicial Politeness'
Signed
Watercolour and bodycolour
12 x 10 inches
Illustrated: *Vanity Fair*, 12 March 1892, Judges no 36, 'Judicial
Politeness'

SPY (SIR LESLIE WARD) (1851-1922)
The Right Honourable Sir Charles Synge Christopher Bowen, PC, DCL, LLD, FRS

After being called to the bar at Lincoln's Inn in 1861, Charles Synge Christopher Bowen first rose to prominence as part of the prosecution team in the Tichborne Case, a cause célèbre that captured the public imagination in the late 1860s and early 1870s. In 1879 he was appointed a High Court judge in the Queen's Bench and in 1882 was raised to the position of Lord Justice of Appeal. In 1893, the year after his portrait appeared in *Vanity Fair*, he was made a Lord of Appeal in Ordinary and a life peer with the title Baron Bowen. In his youth, he played a single first-class cricket match for Hampshire against the MCC. He is credited with coining the phrase 'the man on the Clapham omnibus'.

'Judicial Politeness'

"Born to a Freshwater parson in the Isle of Wight seven-and-fifty years ago, he developed in quite early childhood remarkable talent, physical and mental. He was sent to Rugby, where he won races, played in the Eleven, joined the almost invincible football team, became Captain of the School, and, by way of incidental variation, took the Balliol Scholarship. This last exploit led him to Oxford, where he ran a course whose brilliance is yet uneclipsed. He won the Hertford, the Ireland, and the Latin Verse; he wrote the Arnold Prize Essay, and took First Classes in all his Schools; and, while waiting for his degree, he cantered off with a Balliol Fellowship. He went from Oxford to the Bar; joined the Western Circuit; and having 'devilled' for a space for the present Lord Chief Justice – (thereby improving his master's reputation) – he became Junior Counsel for the Treasury and a made man. He was the Senior Truck Commissioner in 1870; fashioned into Recorder of Penance in 1871; and improved into the most youthful Judge on record before he had taken silk, at forty-four. He has been honoured with a Commemoration degree at Oxford, and he is Visitor of his old College.

As a puisne Judge he was a failure with juries, who could not appreciate his cooing mildness any more than they could his distinctive niceties; but the British juryman is the only thing that he has ever been known to fail with. He has now for ten years been a Lord Justice, unequalled alike for his knowledge of Law and Equity; without rival in his ready grasp of hard cases or his quick solution of intricate problems; all but infallible; and a contriver of judgments that are models for their law, their English, their lucidity, and their strength. He is an unruffled Judge; too modest to be ever contemptuous, yet full of the most polite and gentle sarcasm. He has a masculine intellect, a sweet, low voice, a stupendous memory, a gentle, deprecating manner, and a round, large-eyed face which would do credit to a Bishop.

He is one of the few Judges who are known in Society; of which he is fond without frivolity. He is a cultured man of vast information, who can talk well on all worthy subjects; but he is so unassertive that he has been called shy. He is altogether the best lawyer in England; and when it loses him the Bench will lose its brightest ornament. He belongs to the Athenæum and University Clubs; and he has found time to make a scholarly translation of Virgil's Eclogues and of the First Book of the Aeneid. He has been very ill; but he is now happily progressing towards recovery."

Vanity Fair, 12 March 1892

Lib (Liborio Prosperi) (1854-1928)
Mr Edward Lloyd

As a tenor singer, Edward Lloyd (1845-1927) was considered to be the main successor of Sims Reeves as the country's leading tenor. In 1877, he replaced Sims Reeves for the Handel Triennial Festival at the Crystal Palace and would participate in every subsequent festival until his retirement in 1900. He created many of the great tenor roles in late Victorian oratorio and concert works, such as in *The Martyr of Antioch* in 1880 and Arthur Sullivan's *The Golden Legend* in 1886. He gave is farewell performance at the Royal Albert Hall in 1900, but came out of retirement to sing at the coronation of George V in 1911.

'English Tenor'

"It is seven-and-forty years since he began shrilly to exercise that voice by the gift of which unequal Nature has made him famous. His first notes were heard in the neighbourhood of Kennington; but even at the early age of seven he was too good a vocalist for the mere edification of his humble playmates. So he was promoted from the nursery to the Choir of Westminster Abbey; and being a good, steady little boy, with no greatly developed taste for mischief, he got on, and was presently improved into solo tenor at the St James's Chapel Royal. Then he left the Church to come before the more secular public at Novello's Concerts; and more than twenty years ago he made his mark at a Gloucester Festival where, with the aid of Bach's 'Passion' music, he sang himself into popular favour. Since then he has sung wherever it is worth a man's while to sing; until he has come to be looked upon as the first of English tenors.

He may not be all that Sims Reeves once was; but his artistic excellence is so complete that he can command higher terms for a song than any other English rival. He has made two successful tours, after the modern style, in the United States; and he has but just returned from New York in time to show what he can do in a great part at the Crystal Palace to-day.

He is growing fat."

Vanity Fair, 25 June 1892

48
Lib (Liborio Prosperi) (1854-1928)
Mr Edward Lloyd
'English Tenor'
Signed
Inscribed with title on reverse
Watercolour and bodycolour
12 x 6 ½ inches
Provenance: A G Witherby;
Stanley Jackson;
The John Franks Collection
Illustrated: *Vanity Fair*, 25 June 1892, Men of the Day no 541,
'English Tenor'

SPY (SIR LESLIE WARD) (1851-1922)
Colonel William Cornwallis-West, MP

William Cornwallis-West (1835-1917) was born in Florence, the youngest child of Frederick West of Ruthin Castle, Denbighshire. Following his education – at Eton and Lincoln's Inn – he returned to Florence and developed his talent as a painter, gaining a reputation as a copyist, and also collecting. On the early death of his elder brother, Frederick, in 1868, he succeeded to the estate of Ruthin, and four years later married 17 year-old Mary Fitzpatrick, who would become a leading socialite (and have an affair with the Prince of Wales). They shared their time between Ruthin and 49 Eaton Place.

West became High Sheriff of Denbighshire (1872), Lord-Lieutenant of Denbighshire (1872-1917), a justice of the peace and Honorary Colonel in the 4th battalion of the Royal Welch Fusiliers, and was awarded the Royal Naval Volunteer Reserve Officers' decoration. In 1885 he was returned to parliament for Denbighshire West, a seat he held until 1892, first as a Liberal and then as a Liberal Unionist.

On the death of his mother in 1886, West came into possession of Newlands Manor, Lymington, Hampshire, and attempted to develop the resort of Milford on Sea in emulation of the Duke of Devonshire's project at Eastbourne.

His children included George, who was the second husband of Jennie Jerome, mother of Winston Churchill, and then the second husband of the actress, Mrs Patrick Campbell; Daisy, Princess of Pless; and Constance Edwina, Duchess of Westminster.

'Denbighshire'

"His father and his grandfather are Members of the Lower House; his great grand-father was a member of the Upper House; and his grandmother by judicious attention to business improved Newlands Manor (where he now lives when he is not at Ruthin Castle) into the estate which it now is. He thus began life seven-and-fifty years ago under promising conditions; which he nursed at Eton and at Lincoln's Inn until he burst upon the world of fashion as the husband of a beautiful lady. He has since been made Mayor of Ruthin, High Sheriff and Lord-Lieutenant of Denbighshire, and Honorary Colonel of the 1st Volunteer Battalion Royal Welsh Fusiliers; and having failed to enter Parliament as the chosen of Lymington or of West Cheshire, he began to represent the electors of West Denbighshire in 1885; and is like to be asked to-day to go on representing them so long as the new Parliament or himself shall last.

He has done something for the farmer and a good deal for the labourer by developing Milford-on-Sea, near Lymington, until it is able to support quite a big hotelful of visitors besides a number of residents. He takes an active interest in education; he is a County Councillor of rural Lymington, and, although he is a Liberal, he is a sturdy supporter of the Union. He also, as a man of taste who knows something of Art, promoted a successful Art Treasure Exhibition at Wrexham, which was presided over by the Duke of Westminster. He is a discreet, generous, and hospitable gentleman, and he is the father-in-law of a Prince."

Vanity Fair, 16 July 1892

49
Spy (Sir Leslie Ward) (1851-1922)
Colonel William Cornwallis-West, MP
'Denbighshire'
Signed
Watercolour with bodycolour
15 ½ x 7 ½ inches
Illustrated: *Vanity Fair*, 16 July 1892, Statesmen no 595, 'Denbighshire'

SPY (SIR LESLIE WARD) (1851-1922)
Mr Walter Herries Pollock

The second son of Sir William Frederick Pollock, Walter Herries Pollock (1850-1926) was best known as the editor of the London weekly newspaper, the *Saturday Review*, from 1884 to 1894. On leaving the position, he moved to Chawton to devote himself to his writing and, in 1899, produced a major study of Jane Austen, a previous resident of that Hampshire village. His wide-ranging output included essays, novels, plays and poems, as well as translations from French, and he numbered Egerton Castle and Rudyard Kipling among the members of his wide literary circle. In addition, Pollock participated in the first revival of historical fencing in Britain, and gained repute as the finest amateur fencer in the country. In 1897, he contributed to *Fencing, Boxing and Wrestling* for the Badminton Library of Sports and Pastimes published by Longmans, Green & Company.

'The Saturday Review'

"The second son of that Sir William Frederick Pollock who was Queen's Remembrancer, Senior Master of the Supreme Court of Judicature, and brother to the present Judge, he was born two-and-forty years ago; and with inherited abilities, acquired enough learning at Eton to achieve classical honours at Trinity, Cambridge, by the age of manhood. Three years later he was called to the Bar by the Benchers of the Inner Temple; for by family tradition he was born to the Profession of the Law, so many of whose prizes have been won by the Pollocks this last century. But, like his elder brother (the present Baronet), he affected Letters rather than Briefs; and presently became so accomplished a purveyor of high-class articles that he was added to the staff of The Saturday Review, then the strongest, most slashing, and incisive 'Review of Politics, Literature, Science, and Art' that we had with us. Here he found such room for success, and filled it so capably, that within nine years from his call to the Bar he was improved into Editor of The Saturday; which under him is still the wholesome, scholarly, honest, and high-class Tory paper that it was when he first wrote for it. He has been guilty of several little books, and he still finds time to write more; he has a pretty knack of versifying; he knows French and the French; and he is possessed with all the strength of his opinions.

He is a rather grave, quiet man, and an accomplished master of fence who handles the foils as no other English gentleman can handle them in these degenerate days. He is a great believer in the short story; and he has only not perpetrated a three-volume novel because, not being a journalist, he is unable, with all his literary skill, to 'pad.' Yet he means some day to put all the dogs, cats, birds, and other animals that he has known into a book that shall be written on the lines of Théophile Gautier's 'Ménagerie Intime'; for he has been a student and friend of these creatures from his childhood, and he greatly admires the style of the French Master. He has been called a Model of Grace and Breeding; and he has the look and the carriage of an Aristocrat."

Vanity Fair, 31 December 1892

50
Spy (Sir Leslie Ward) (1851-1922)
Mr Walter Herries Pollock
'The Saturday Review'
Signed
Watercolour with bodycolour and pencil on tinted paper
12 ¾ x 7 ¾ inches
Illustrated: *Vanity Fair*, 31 December 1892, Men of the Day no 553, 'The Saturday Review'

SPY (SIR LESLIE WARD) (1851-1922)
Mr Fred Crisp

Fred Crisp (1849-1905) made his fortune owning a large number of shops on the Seven Sisters Road in London, before turning his attention to farming and breeding champion shire horses and Highland cattle.

'He Owns "Chancellor"'

"Born of humble stock, he came into the world some two-and-forty years ago; arriving first in Cambridgeshire, whence he came to London and began to make money. He bought and sold drapery and other articles of domestic commerce until he became the Maple of the northern suburbs with an emporium in the Seven Sisters Road. When he had made money he took to farming land, breeding Shire horses and exhibiting them at all the chief shows; and he is like to be well in evidence this month at the Agricultural Show at Chester. He bought the famous mare, Starlight, and won the Lockinge Challenge Shield for Shire horses for the third successive time last year. He owned Chancellor, for which great stallion he gave eleven hundred guineas. He has even been privileged to sell Shire horses and Highland-bred cattle to the Queen and to the Prince of Wales; for he has a fine show of Shorthorns. He owns several farms, and he sells stock at Southgate, where he has sixty acres of land and a mile or two of glass. He has been seen with the hounds, and he has been asked to stand for Parliament.

He dresses very beautifully."

Vanity Fair, 8 June 1893

51
SPY (SIR LESLIE WARD) (1851-1922)
Mr Fred Crisp
'He Owns "Chancellor"'
Signed
Watercolour and bodycolour on tinted paper
15 x 10 inches
Provenance: A G Witherby;
Stanley Jackson;
The John Franks Collection
Illustrated: *Vanity Fair*, 8 June 1893, Men of the Day no 567,
'He Owns "Chancellor"'
Exhibited: 'Vanity Fair 1869-1914', Church Farm House Museum,
Hendon, September-December 1983

SPY (SIR LESLIE WARD) (1851-1922)
Mr William Allan, MP

Born into a working class family in Dundee, Sir William Allan joined the Royal Navy as an engineer, during which time he served aboard a ship engaged in the American Civil War. In 1886, he started his own engineering company in Sunderland, the Scotia Engine Works, after reviving the fortunes of the North-Eastern Engineering Company in his role as manager. In February 1893 he became Liberal MP for Gateshead, which he held until his death in 1903.

'The Gateshead Giant'

"Of humble stock, Scotch, sturdy, canny, thrifty, he made his entrance on this stage some fifty 'or thereby' years ago. But of his origin little is known, save that he throve on porridge. In which respect he later came to feel the potent consequence of sound oatmeal on literary culture. For, though bound apprentice to an engineer, he found spare moments for the Muse. To get, maybe, still more beyond his depth he went to sea: lived hard, showed grit, and wooed that fickle jade, Fortune-so-called-by running the blockade. Sea-serpents, cyclones, mermaids, and the rest, mixed up with hair-breadth 'scapes, enriched his quest for bold adventure… Ultimately, tired of wandering, the sailor-bard was hired to 'boss' some engineering works up North; whence, after long seclusion, he came forth, a full-fledged Radical authority, chosen by Gateshead's 868 majority, to shut his eyes and vote by crack of whip as Caucuses might order: to a chip of Scottish block, distracting!

Yet this bluff and rugged poetaster has good stuff. Warm-hearted, horny handed, ex-mechanic; big-limbed, big-bearded, big-voiced, and Titanic; although his glare is savagely defiant, he is a genial kind of Gateshead Giant, whose faults are on the surface.

Only those who know his verses thank him for his prose."

Vanity Fair, 26 October 1893

52
SPY (SIR LESLIE WARD) (1851-1922)
Mr William Allan, MP
'The Gateshead Giant'
Signed
Inscribed with title on reverse
Watercolour and bodycolour
13 x 7 inches
Illustrated: *Vanity Fair*, 26 October 1893, Statesmen no 623,
'The Gateshead Giant'

SPY (SIR LESLIE WARD) (1851-1922)
'At Cowes'

'The R.Y.S.'

The Yacht Club was founded in St James's, London, on 1 June 1815 as a club for gentlemen interested in yachting. Membership was restricted to those who owned a vessel 'not under' 10 tons and members would meet in London and in Cowes, Isle of Wight, twice a year. In 1817, the Prince Regent became a member and in 1820, when he was crowned George IV, it was renamed the Royal Yacht Club.

In 1826, the Royal Yacht Club began organising racing as the principal feature of the annual regatta at Cowes (now known as Cowes Week), the winning prize being a gold cup valued at £100.

In 1833, William IV renamed the club The Royal Yacht Squadron. In 1851, the club's commodore visited the Great Exhibition in Hyde Park, London, and issued a challenge for the RYS Cup, in a race around the Isle of Wight. The New York-based vessel, *America*, representing the New York Yacht Club, won the race, thus giving its name to what is now one of the oldest and most famous sporting trophies, the America's Cup.

Published in *Vanity Fair*'s Winter Supplement of 1894, this preliminary drawing and lithograph (see page 111) features six members of the Squadron in discussion at Cowes.

Portrayed opposite from left to right:

German Emperor and King of Prussia Wilhelm II (1859-1941). Elected a member in 1889, Kaiser Wilhelm was an active participant in the annual regatta in the 1890s. In 1891, he had purchased the America's Cup challenger, *Thistle*, renamed her *Meteor*, and in 1893 won the Squadron Regatta Cup.

The Earl of Dunraven, Windham Thomas Wyndham-Quin (1841-1926). A Peer from 1871, Dunraven sat in the House of Lords and was a close ally of Lord Randolph Churchill, writing pamplets on the Irish Question and serving as President of the Fair Trade League. He served as Under-Secretary for the Colonies in Lord Salisbury's administration in 1885-6 and again in 1886-7. However, Dunraven was chiefly known to the public as a yachtsman and was often criticised for neglecting his political duties for yachting. He competed for the America's Cup on behalf of the RYS in 1893 and 1895 with two specially built yachts, *Valkyrie II* and *Valkyrie III* – both times unsuccessfully.

Rear Admiral the Hon. Victor Montagu (1841-1915). A Godson of Queen Victoria, Victor Montagu joined the Royal Navy aged 11 and saw action during the Crimean War and the Indian Mutiny, before being promoted to captain in 1877 and taking command of HMS Garnet in 1882. He retired from active service in 1885 and in 1892, whilst retired, was promoted to rear admiral. As a member of the RYS, he designed several boats, including the Montagu Whaler in 1890, which would become the standard sea boat of the Royal Navy from 1910 to 1970.

HRH Edward, Prince of Wales (1841-1910). A keen yachtsman since his youth, the Prince of Wales had been a member of the RYS since 1863, before accepting the office of Commodore in 1882. In 1893, the Prince of Wales had unveiled the new vessel *Britannia*, considered to be one of the finest racing ships ever built. During *Britannia*'s first five seasons, she entered 219 races and won 147 prizes. When he ascended the throne as Edward VII in 1901 he resigned his position as Commodore, but retained his association with the RYS as its Admiral.

The 3rd Marquess of Ormonde, James Edward William Theobald Butler (1844-1919). The last Marquess of Ormonde to live at Kilkenny Castle, James Butler was a keen yachtsman and a close friend of Edward VII. The owner of several large ships, he had become a member of the RYS in 1867. He held the position of Vice-Commodore of the RYS from 1885 until 1901, when he succeeded King Edward as Commodore.

The 5th Earl of Londsale, Hugh Cecil Lowther (1857-1944). A keen sportsman from a young age, the Earl of Lonsdale was known as a leading proponent of boxing and its recognition as a sport. In 1888, he travelled to Canada and then on to the Arctic Circle by horse, boat and dog sleigh. He reappeared in San Francisco in April 1889 by way of northern Alaska. He arrived back in England as a celebrity and in 1891 became a founder and the first President of the National Sporting Club. As a member of the RYS, Londsale raced with Lord Dunraven aboard the *Valkyrie* and purchased his own yacht, *Dierdré*, in 1893 from Dunraven. In 1894, it was aboard his next vessel, *Shamrock*, that he entertained the German Emperor during his visit to Cowes.

53
Spy (Sir Leslie Ward) (1851-1922)
'At Cowes
The R.Y.S.'
Watercolour and pencil
12 ¼ x 17 inches
Illustrated: Preliminary drawing for *Vanity Fair*, 6 December 1894,
Winter Supplement, 'At Cowes: The R.Y.S.'

The R.Y.S.

"Of all the booths that are to be found in this great Fair, there is none that is so hard to enter as the Royal Yacht Squadron; nor any to which admission is more prized even by the most high-placed. For, to use modern jargon, membership of the Squadron gives 'cachet' which is not to be had otherwise. Yachting, in the Cowes Season, is the sport of Kings – and millionaires. The humbler person may own a yacht and may make a seaman, and may do most venturous things and get much delight thereout; yet it is not for him to gain admittance within the Castle portals because only he is a good seaman, or a good yachtsman, or a bold fellow. He must be much else before he shall be entitled to fly the White Ensign. On the other hand, he need not be all that is bold and seamanlike in order to attain the high Cowes degree. Wicked men have said that sailing and the ability to sail are but an accident in the composition of a few members of the Royal Yacht Squadron; but plainly this is to go too far. Many an old Viking has set sail from Cowes Roads in a breeze that might urge a racing cutter with all her canvas spread through the water at the rate of quite six knots; has so ventured outside; has actually, greatly daring, circumnavigated the Island and yet lived to tell the tale of stays, and tacks, and green seas which might have come aboard had his ship been less skilfully handled by his gold lace-capped skipper. Such daring cruises have been done by the Squadron men of old; and now the Castle is fuller of brave spirits than ever it has been. When the Commodore became owner of the fastest cutter afloat he gave great impetus to yacht-racing; and most members of the Yacht Squadron now look upon racing with real interest, while the rest pretend to do so in respectful admiration of their Commodore's British pluck.

Once in each year there comes Holy Week at Cowes; when the little place is so crowded that a lodging ashore – for all who go down to Cowes do not go down in ships – may cost as much for a week as it may for other ten weeks. It is at this time that the Garden of the Royal Yacht Squadron is gaped at by miserable outsiders as the Holy of Holies of Fashion; to gain entrance to which fair Dames will do what they will scarce do for any other thing or man. The lucky or deserving among them enter this paradise daily and sit on chairs that are perched upon the uncomfortable grassy slope, full of determined anxiety to meet and touch the hand of that Royalty whom they have been meeting all through the just finished Season. These ladies, arrayed in all their glory, make a beautiful sight, such as may be seen nowhere else the world over; while the men are all nautical – very nautical. Blue suits topped by yachting caps and bottomed by yellow shoes are everywhere. Gold lace, badges, emblems, symbols, and the letters 'R.Y.S.,' are at this time common objects of the Cowes sea-shore. It is even said that some worthy members have these mystic letters tattooed on their persons. But it would be wrong to suppose that all the letters and badges and emblems combined could make, or prove, one seaman. Yet some of these blue-coated fellows are England's best men, real sailors, enterprising yachtsmen, good sportsmen; for the English still love the sea, and yachting is brave sport.

Let us look at some of these, as they kept the Holy Week this year. There is first His Royal Highness the Prince of Wales; most popular of Englishmen, most actual sportsman after the British manner, and owner of the Britannia. Much has the Prince done for yachting; much more for the Royal Yacht Squadron; even more for English sport. The English sportsman will not win a race by all means possible. He would rather be beaten than win ingloriously. Nor, when he is beaten by foreign resources that himself would disdain to use, will he object to the winning boat. He will win against all dodges, or he will take a beating; for his notions of what sport should be are English notions, not American, and solid. Of such is our Prince of Wales.

There is foreign Royalty in the Garden. The German Emperor is a new yachtsman; who is nevertheless an authority on yachting. For he is an Admirable Crichton, who does everything well, from alarming one of his own garrisons in time of peace to composing an opera; from racing a yacht on the sea to correcting the decision of a Hanging Committee in an Art Gallery. He is a universal expert, who can do everything; and he does everything. He is very full of enthusiasm, and he is really learning to be a yachtsman. Moreover he has won the Queen's Cup with the Meteor. He has learned much at Cowes and has enjoyed much; so that he means to come again.

Descended from the first Chief Butler of Ireland – who died nearly seven hundred years ago – Lord Ormonde is of the 'old salt' breed, who loves the sea and all that on it is. He has done a great deal of yachting, but no yacht-racing; he is one of the few unprofessional sailors who holds a certificate from the Board of Trade to command his own ship; and he is so good a seaman that he despises the modern racing machine. He is indeed so smart a sailor that he makes sailors of others, keeping up quite naval discipline on board his ship. All his yachts have been Mirages; but there is nothing at all deceptive about their owner.

Lord Dunraven has but one mirage – a fading prospect of winning the America's Cup. He has tried very hard, and he has deserved, even though he has not commanded, success: and doing so, he has gained the respect of all as a thorough sportsman of patriotic intent. He is a very keen yachting man who knows all about a yacht. He is also the holder of a certificate, and he is a very hard-headed fellow. If the Americans will accept fair conditions, he is ready to build another Watson boat that shall be better than the ill-fated Valkyrie, and that shall be meant to take the wind out of any American's sails and give him a stern chase home. He can do more than own a yacht, as he showed in his last season's twenty-rater, whose lines were designed absolutely, if unsuccessfully, by her owner. He called her Audrey; for she was all 'his own'; and, like Touchstone's Audrey, she was 'an ill-favoured thing.' He has done much besides yachting. Since he earned popularity as an officer in the Household Brigade by riding steeplechases, he has been a special war correspondent, a Colonial Secretary, a Royal Commissioner to inquire into a big subject, and an author of reputable works on the Soudan, Irish Architecture, 'The Great Divide,' and Free Trade. He is, moreover, an authority on hunting; and he is filled with ambition.

Lord Lonsdale has long been known as a plucky sportsman ashore. He is lately become a recruit of the yacht-racing world; and though he knows little about it yet, he will learn. He bought the twenty-rater Deirdre from Lord Dunraven, and did well with her last season; but he did not sail her himself, nor, indeed, did he often sail in her.

Admiral Montagu is another keen yachtsman; but being the good seaman that he is, he knows little of yachts, less of yacht-racing, and will not learn. His is a very genial figure at all the Regattas, and all men like him. He has done much to keep up the forty-rating class with his three ships, Vendetta, Corsair, and Carina.

There are many others in this Royal Yacht Squadron booth; sailors, seamen, yachtsmen, yachting men, longshoremen, picknickers, millionaires who have much to recommend them, and millioniares who have nothing but their millions. But the wrong members are few, and the improving Squadron is the best-manned Club in all Vanity Fair."

Vanity Fair, 6 December 1894

SPY (SIR LESLIE WARD) (1851-1922)
Mr Clement King Shorter

A journalist and editor, Clement King Shorter began his career as a sub-editor for the *Penny Illustrated Paper* and columnist for *The Star* whilst working as a clerk in the Exchequer and Audit Department at Somerset House. In 1891, following the retirement of the editor of the *Illustrated London News*, John Lash Latey, Shorter offered himself to the director, William Ingram, for the role and was accepted. Together with Ingram, he founded and became editor of *The Sketch* in 1892 and, following its acquisition by Ingram in 1893, editor of *The English Illustrated Magazine*. In the years following his appearance in *Vanity Fair*, he would become founder and editor of *The Sphere* (1900) and *Tatler* (1901).

'Three Editors'

"Born in London, he was sent to school at Downham Market in Norfolk, where they whipped into him the elements of grammar. Then he wasted a year or two variously (the only wasted years of his life), tired of it, and went to Somerset House as a Civil Service clerk in the Exchequer and Audit Department. He thinks that he made a bad Clerk; but in the course of seven years he acquired a knowledge of figures that made him quite a Man of Letters; which he showed by writing. He edited a selection of Wordsworth's Poems, and he wrote a biography of Charlotte Brontë. He further improved the public time and his own fortunes by writing of literature in The Star when it first began to shine under Mr. T. P. O'Connor; and Mr. H. W. Massingham (who knew him from his Norfolk days), invited him to join the staff: which he did as the inconsequent scribbler of 'Books and Bookmen.' Then other Editors asked him for work, till he was doing more outside Somerset House than he ever did in it. Presently he heard that Mr. Latey was retiring from the editorship of The Illustrated London News, and being a man who believes in not missing chances he forthwith called upon Mr. William Ingram and offered to take the vacant chair; and Mr. Ingram was too amazed at his impudence to decline the offer. That was four years ago, and since then Mr. William Ingram has become Sir William, and Mr. Shorter has become three Editors at once. For two years back the pair evolved The Sketch, of which the very successful idea was the definite application of photography to journalism; and that bold venture (which paid within a year) made him a second Editor, whose staircase has since been almost daily thronged by 'ladies of the profession.' Finally, when Sir William Ingram bought The English Illustrated Magazine, he naturally became a third Editor; so that he is now responsible for three illustrated periodicals, each one of which would be enough to satisfy the industry of a bigger man.

He is instance of the born Editor; for he never learned his business, yet gets through it most competently. He is an active fellow who grapples with much work quickly, yet refrains from offending people, even when he is most busy; for like most very busy men he can always find five minutes to spare. He has travelled a good deal – westerly to Chicago, easterly to Rumania and elsewhere; and when he travels he sees things. He has made many friends and a few enemies; and it is said of him that he is only disliked by those who are jealous of him because he has no business to be three Editors in one. He is a good-natured, genial, friendly person; who is still full of projects."

Vanity Fair, 24 December 1894

54
SPY (SIR LESLIE WARD) (1851-1922)
Mr Clement King Shorter
'Three Editors'
Signed
Inscribed 'Clement Shorter Esq' below mount
Watercolour with bodycolour on tinted paper
11 ½ x 7 inches
Illustrated: *Vanity Fair*, 24 December 1894, Men of the Day no 607,
'Three Editors'

SPY (SIR LESLIE WARD) (1851-1922)
Mr Samuel Whitbread

Born into a family of brewers, Samuel Whitbread (1830-1915) began his political career in 1850 as Private Secretary to the Governor of New Zealand, Sir George Grey. In 1852 he was elected MP for Bedford and held the seat until 1895. From 1859 to 1863 he was Civil Lord of the Admiralty.

'Parliamentary Procedure'

"Son of the late Samuel Charles Whitbread, M.P. for Cardington, and grandson of the well-known politician, he was born to wholesome estate five-and-sixty years ago; and after doing Rugby and Trinity, Cambridge, he became Private Secretary to Sir George Grey. At the age of two-and-twenty he was chosen to sit for Bedford Borough; and for Bedford he kept sitting until just now, when he retired and his constituency was swamped, like the best part of the country, by a very welcome wave of Toryism. Yet he sat very successfully. When a Member of three years' standing he married a daughter of the third Earl of Chichester; then he became Civil Lord of the Admiralty; and during his forty-two years of Parliament it is said on the best possible authority that he was three times asked to be Speaker. He is a very wealthy brewer who is now Chairman of Whitbread and Company; and a Deputy-Lieutenant, a Justice of the Peace, and a County Alderman of Bedfordshire. He is also a Gladstonian in whom there is no guile.

He has always been much better known in the House than outside of it; and there he has long had reputation as an authority on Parliamentary Procedure. He has also been generally recognised as a speaker of words which carried much weight with the Liberal Party; though flippant Tories have regarded him as the heavy father of light comedy. He has a paternal manner, and he brims over with virtuous sayings; which also have been flippantly called platitudes. He has always shown himself ready to play the impartial judge in any Parliamentary row; and he has justified himself in the role by always deciding in favour of his own side. For he is a good fellow as well as a good man of business."

Vanity Fair, 8 August 1895

55
SPY (SIR LESLIE WARD) (1851-1922)
Mr Samuel Whitbread
'Parliamentary Procedure'
Signed
Inscribed with title on reverse
Watercolour and bodycolour
14 x 7 inches
Illustrated: *Vanity Fair*, 8 August 1895, Men of the Day no 626, 'Parliamentary Procedure'

SPY (SIR LESLIE WARD) (1851-1922)
The Earl of Eglinton and Winton

George Arnulph Montgomerie (1848-1919) was the 15th Earl of Eglinton and 3rd Earl of Winton. His father, Archibald William Montgomerie, had been a passionate devotee of racing and his creation of the Eglinton Tournament, a vast medieval tournament and banquet held in 1839, had made him one of the most popular noblemen in Scotland. George Arnulph Montgomerie also became a keen sportsman and regularly participated at the Wimbledon Championships between 1878 and 1887, even advancing to the semi-finals in 1880.

'A Good Sportsman'

"George Arnulph Montgomerie, the fifteenth Earl of his house, who was born seven-and-forty years ago, comes of a family so ancient that he can trace his lineage back to Robert of Montgomery; who is believed to have been descended from Roger of Mundegumbri, one of the Conqueror's Norman nobles, who was made Earl of Shrewsbury. Quite naturally, therefore, he went to Eton; but he did so unusually, at the early age of seven. There he became Captain of the Lower School Football; and at thirteen, on the death of his father, he left school; though he did not succeed his brother, the late Earl, until he was four-and-forty. He is a capital rider who began early; for he hunted by himself at the age of nine with the Ward Union Staghounds; his father being then Lord-Lieutenant. After Eton, he quite properly took up the profession of killing and joined the Grenadier Guards; so that he was in Dublin at the time of the Fenian riots. Altogether an accomplished sportsman, he won the garrison Hundred Yards race in Dublin; rode much, chiefly in steeplechases; and did it so well that he once beat H. Grimshaw in a six-furlong welter at Liverpool – by a short head. He is one of the best hunting men in the kingdom; who, on his brother's death, kept the Earl of Eglinton's Hounds; which he still hunts in Ayrshire. He is also a good shot, who once hit two-and-thirty driven grouse in three-and-thirty shots. More seriously, he is Hereditary Sheriff of Renfrew, and Deputy-Lieutenant for Ayrshire; and so he commands general respect.

He has a cheerful, genial manner; he is a gentleman as well as a good sportsman and a kindly man; and he is generally liked."

Vanity Fair, 16 January 1896

56
SPY (SIR LESLIE WARD) (1851-1922)
The Earl of Eglinton and Winton
'A Good Sportsman'
Signed
Watercolour and bodycolour on tinted paper
13 ¼ x 8 inches
Provenance: Thomas Gibson Bowles;
Stanley Jackson;
The John Franks Collection
Illustrated: *Vanity Fair*, 16 January 1896, Statesmen no 663,
'A Good Sportsman'
Exhibited: 'Vanity Fair 1869-1914', Church Farm House Museum,
Hendon, September-December 1983

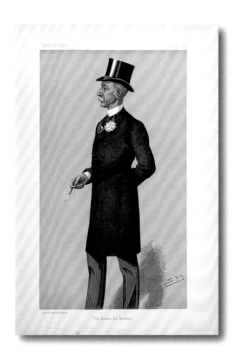

SPY (SIR LESLIE WARD) (1851-1922)
Sir Lewis McIver, Bart, MP

Sir Lewis McIver (1846-1920) was a Liberal politician who first entered the Commons as MP for Torquay in 1885. He lost this seat the following year and joined the Liberal Unionist Party. In 1895 he stood successfully for Edinburgh West and held the seat until his resignation in 1909.

'The Member For Scotland'

"John McIver, Secretary of the Presidency Bank in Madras, became his father half a century ago; and having learned what he might at school and at Bonn University, he became a Barrister eighteen years back, while he was yet in the Indian Civil Service. He has held a dozen various positions, such as that of Under-Secretary, to the Government in Burma, of Chief Magistrate in Rangoon, of Magistrate in the Nilgiri District, and of Registrar of the High Court; and he is President of the London, Ross, and Cromarty Association. Eleven years ago he sat for Torquay; and last year he was the chosen of the West Division of Edinburgh: for he is a wholesome Liberal-Unionist, who though he stands six feet is every inch a patriot.

His Queen honoured him with a Baronetcy on her last birthday; and he is commonly supposed to have deserved it. Though he is only at present in his third Session, his figure and his frock-coat and his virtue make him something of a feature in the House. In the Session of '85 he was famous for his speeches; in the Session of '95 he has been equally famous for his silence. For he is a man of variety in his life, as he has shown. Five-and-twenty years ago he was among the best waltzers in town; now he is among the best speakers in Scotland. He is an all-round sportsman who has given much attention to Friendly Societies; of the best of which he is an honorary member. His seventeen years in India have shown him how great England is, and he has been all over Scotland piping for his Party and for his country; wherefore he is known as the 'Member for Scotland.' He is also well known at bazaars, at football matches, at tea-fights, and at Ranelagh.

He has been called a connection of Mr. Gladstone; yet he is a hot Unionist. He likes paradox; for, having been everywhere, he knows the world. He is a genial fellow who has a future."

Vanity Fair, 23 July 1896

57
Spy (Sir Leslie Ward) (1851-1922)
Sir Lewis McIver, Bart, MP
'The Member For Scotland'
Signed
Watercolour with bodycolour
13 x 8 ¼ inches
Provenance: A G Witherby; Stanley Jackson
Illustrated: *Vanity Fair*, 23 July 1896, Statesmen no 674,
'The Member For Scotland'
Exhibited: 'Vanity Fair 1869-1914', Church Farm House Museum,
Hendon, September-December 1983

SPY (SIR LESLIE WARD) (1851-1922)
Mr John Gilbert Talbot, MP, DCL

John Gilbert Talbot (1835-1910) began his career as Conservative MP for Kent West, a seat he held from 1868 to 1878, when he resigned to fight a by-election in the Oxford University constituency. Emerging victorious, he held the seat until 1910. From 1878 to 1880, he served as Parliamentary Secretary to the Board of Trade under Benjamin Disraeli and in 1897, when his caricature appeared in *Vanity Fair*, he was sworn of the Privy Council.

'Oxford University'

"The late John Chetwynd Talbot, Q.C., became his father two-and-sixty years ago, and his wife was born Miss Meriel Sarah Lyttelton; so that he is an Earl's nephew and a Baron's son-in-law. From the Charterhouse he went to the House (at Oxford); and thence, after two miscarriages (at Kidderminster and Malmesbury), to the House at Westminster. There he sat for nearly thirty years – ten being devoted to the services of West Kent, and the last nineteen to those of the Church, as one of the Members for Oxford University. He was once Secretary to the Board of Trade (under Lord Beaconsfield); and he is a Justice of the Peace for Sussex, Middlesex, and London; a Justice of the Peace, Deputy Lieutenant, and County Councillor for Kent; an Ecclesiastical Commissioner; Chairman of the West Kent Quarter Sessions, and of a Building Company; and a Director of one or two other concerns.

He is an Honorary D.C.L. of Oxford, where he is held in high esteem as a sound Churchman of known principles. Full of zeal, he is always to be heard in any discussion affecting the Church, while his equanimity outside Church matters is striking. He is a brother of the late Warden of Keble.

He is not beautiful, but he is a very well fitted representative of a great Conservative Institution."

Vanity Fair, 8 July 1897

58
SPY (SIR LESLIE WARD) (1851-1922)
Mr John Gilbert Talbot, MP, DCL
'Oxford University'
Signed
Inscribed with title and dated 1897 on reverse
Watercolour and bodycolour on tinted paper
13 ½ x 8 ½ inches
Provenance: A G Witherby;
The John Franks Collection
Illustrated: *Vanity Fair*, 8 July 1897, Statesmen no 687, 'Oxford University'
Exhibited: 'Vanity Fair 1869-1914', Church Farm House Museum, Hendon, September-December 1983

JEAN BAPTISE GUTH (1883-1921)
Major Ferdinand Esterhazy

In 1897, Charles-Marie-Ferdinand Esterhazy (1847-1923), a major in the French army, was revealed as a traitor, having attempted to defect to the German Empire. The revelation ended a scandal that had intrigued observers in Paris and in London since 1894 and had resulted in the false imprisonment of a fellow soldier, Captain Albert Dreyfus. In 1898, shortly after his caricature appeared in *Vanity Fair*, he fled to England, where he would live under a variety of aliases.

'Major Esterhazy'

"A Hungarian family provided two Generals for the French army under the second Empire; to one of whom Count Marie Charles Ferdinand Walsin Esterhazy became son one-and-forty years ago. Naturally, he entered the Service; and in twenty years or so was promoted Chef de Bataillon of the 74th of the Line. He had already smelled powder in the winter of 1870, and in the Tunisian Expedition; and he had been attached to the War Minister.
Six years ago he was mixed up in the memorable duel between Captain Cremieu Foa and Edouard Drumont; he is allied by marriage with one of the oldest families in Lorraine; and he has recently acquired a quite sudden notoriety by implication in l'Affaire Dreyfus: of which, perhaps, more will be heard. He has been heard to say that he does not love Zola.

He is a spare, nervous, well-hated man, with a drooping nose; whose face and swarthy complexion betray his race."

Vanity Fair, 26 May 1898

59
Jean Baptise Guth (1883-1921)
Major Ferdinand Esterhazy
'Major Esterhazy'
Signed and dated 98
Watercolour and bodycolour
12 ½ x 7 inches
Provenance: A G Witherby;
The John Franks Collection
Illustrated: *Vanity Fair*, 26 May 1898, Men of the Day no 714,
'Major Esterhazy'

SPY (SIR LESLIE WARD) (1851-1922)
Lord Farquhar

Horace Farquhar (1844-1923) was a successful banker turned politician, who at the time of his caricature in *Vanity Fair* in 1898, had been raised to the peerage of Baron Farquhar of Marylebone. By the 1890s he had become considerably wealthy through his success in the City, first as manager of Forbes, Forbes & Co. and then as a partner in the private banking house of Sir Samuel Scott, Bart & Co. In 1895 he became MP for Marylebone, a seat he held until he moved to the House of Lords in 1898.

'Horace'

"It is four-and-fifty years since Horace Brand Townsend Farquhar became the fifth son of Sir Walter Minto Townsend Farquhar, M.P., and second Baronet of the Mauritius; and since then he has been many things. His elder brother being a sixth Baronet, he became a first on his own account half-a-dozen years ago; and now he has been improved into a Peer. He is also a Justice of the Peace and Deputy-Lieutenant for Middlesex, a County Councillor for London, President of the London Municipal Society, and heir-presumptive to his brother. He was Member of Parliament for a Marylebone Division before he was translated; he was a partner in the banking firm of Sir Samuel Scott and Co. till they were amalgamated with Parrs, which he now helps to direct; and he was an original Director of the British South Africa Company which has added so much to the Empire.

His father began life in diplomacy, and took an active part in Hertfordshire politics; but himself being without inheritance adopted a business career. At twenty-one he was taken into partnership by Sir Charles Forbes; and for some years he was managing partner of the firm, as well as of the West-End banking house, of Sir Samuel Scott and Co. Since he took to public life he has devoted himself to London politics, dress, and municipal matters; his chief achievement being the foundation of the London Municipal Society, whose President he is. He has represented East Marylebone on the London County Council since there was such a thing; and West Marylebone in the House of Commons. His amusements are Art, shooting, deer-stalking and racing. He is the husband of the widow of the late Sir Edward Scott; and altogether he is a very fortunate, cheerful, well-dressed fellow, who is quite satisfied with himself.

He is well known in London, and everybody calls him 'Horace'."

Vanity Fair, 2 June 1898

60
SPY (SIR LESLIE WARD) (1851-1922)
Lord Farquhar
'Horace'
Signed
Inscribed with title on reverse
Watercolour and bodycolour with pencil
13 x 7 ½ inches
Illustrated: *Vanity Fair*, 2 June 1898, Statesmen no 695, 'Horace'

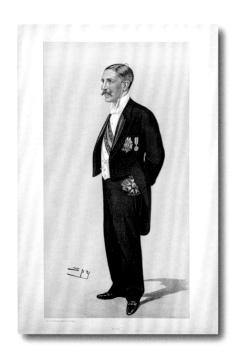

SPY (SIR LESLIE WARD) (1851-1922)
The Hon. Sir Walter Francis Hely-Hutchinson, GCMG

Trained as a barrister, Sir Walter Francis Hely-Hutchinson was a diplomat who spent much of his career aborad, serving in Fiji, Malta and the Caribbean, before being appointed Governor and Commander-in-Chief of Natal and Zululand in 1893, a post he was holding when his portrait appeared in *Vanity Fair*. In 1901, he was appointed Governor of the Cape Colony. Spy depicts Sir Walter Hely-Hutchinson wearing the regalia of the Most Distinguished Order of St Michael and St George.

'Natal'

"He began it in Dublin, nearly half a century ago, by becoming the second son of the fourth Earl of Donoughmore, and the great-great-grandson of that John Hely-Hutchinson who was at once Secretary of State for Ireland and Provost of Trinity College, Dublin. Like all good Irishmen he left Ireland; and having learned what they could teach him at Harrow he went to Cambridge, took his degree in Law and naturally thought of the Bar. He read with A. B. Dickson and Northmore Lawrence in Lincoln's Inn and was not called because the present Lord Donoughmore invited him to his wedding in Hobart: which invitation he accepted at thirty-six hours' notice. In Australia he met Lord Rosmead (then Sir Hercules Robinson) and went with him, as Attaché to the Mission to annex Fiji; after which Sir Hercules made a Private Secretary of him. Twenty years ago he was improved into Colonial Secretary of Barbadoes, after which he got himself called to the Bar. Being thus qualified for work, and still unbriefed, he has successively been Chief Secretary to the Government in Malta, Governor of the Windward Islands, and the first Governor of Natal and Zululand; which last he became five years ago under the new régime.

He has only spent twenty-three months of the last quarter of a century in England; yet are his friends in this country not tired of him. He is, indeed, one of the most popular of men; for he is a good fellow, an honest sportsman, a capital story-teller, and full of tact. He is also a man of judgment, with a knack of getting on with strangers. In Natal – whither he returned on Saturday after a short visit to England – he is as popular as he is in England. He is a good polo-player and a keen golfer who has played cricket; he can shoot, and his performances in the saddle are still remembered in Tipperary, Curraghmore, and Kilkenny. He is so well informed that he can talk with most men on their own subjects; besides which he is quite an authority on drainage. He is also a good speaker who has a sense of humour; a domesticated husband who is devoted to a charming wife, and an unaffected, good fellow."

Vanity Fair, 7 July 1898

61
SPY (SIR LESLIE WARD) (1851-1922)
The Hon. Sir Walter Francis Hely-Hutchinson, GCMG
'Natal'
Signed
Watercolour with bodycolour on tinted paper
6 ¾ x 12 ¼ inches
Illustrated: *Vanity Fair*, 7 July 1898, Men of the Day no 717, 'Natal'

SPY (SIR LESLIE WARD) (1851-1922)
The Chevalier De Souza Correa

João Arthur de Souza Corrêa (c1840-1900) was the Brazilian Ambassador to the United Kingdom, serving from 1890 until his death in 1900.

'Brazil'

"He is Envoy-Extraordinary and Minister Plenipotentiary accredited by Brazil to the Court of St James. He is also the doyen of the Corps Diplomatique in London; whither he was first appointed, more than a quarter of a century ago, as Attaché to the Brazilian Legation. Having resided among us for so long he has become quite endeared to us; and it is commonly believed that he likes the English almost as well as they like him. Since 1890 – when he was transferred from Rome – he has been Secretary and Minister to London; but popular as he is amongst us, he is still a bachelor. He is well liked by all – from the highest to the lowest; and he is so much identified with English life that you meet him everywhere – at Court in the best Clubs, in country houses, at the Opera, and at races. He has many friends, and he is always as welcome at the Foreign Office as he is at Hatfield.

He is fond of music; he is a very well-informed man, and he is a real friend to England."

Vanity Fair, 18 August 1898

62
Spy (Sir Leslie Ward) (1851-1922)
The Chevalier De Souza Correa
'Brazil'
Signed
Inscribed with title on reverse
Watercolour and bodycolour on tinted paper
13 x 8 inches
Provenance: A G Witherby;
The John Franks Collection
Illustrated: *Vanity Fair*, 18 August 1898, Men of the Day no 722,
'Brazil'

JEAN BAPTISE GUTH (1883-1921)
M. Théophile Delcassé

Théophile Delcassé (1852-1923) was a French statesman, whose caricatured appeared in *Vanity Fair* shortly after he had been named as the French Foreign Minister. Strongly anti-German, he improved relations between France and Italy and France and Russia, before concluding the Entente Cordiale with Great Britain in April 1904.

'French Foreign Affairs'

"The journalist in France gets on oftener than he does out of France: because, on doubt, he is a cleverer fellow. So when Théophile had been named − (which happened at Pamiers seven-and-forty years ago) − he naturally began his career as a scribbler for newspapers. Now he is something like the biggest man in France. The years are only ten since he was first elected to the Chamber; four years later he became Under-Secretary for the French Colonies (such as they are); and after the fall of the Méline Cabinet last year M. Brisson improved him into Minister for Foreign Affairs, and so brought him into very direct conflict with our own Lord Salisbury. He did not achieve Fashoda, but he dealt with that little matter so diplomatically that he retains his Portfolio in M. Dupuy's Ministry − though the Brisson Administration has been defeated. For he is a very clever fellow, even among Frenchmen; who can look very firm even after he has decided to yield to the inevitable.

He is not a big man physically, but behind his glasses his eyes gleam with lively interrogation. He has the gift of speaking, and he is a robust fighter in debates, and the most implacable man in the Méline Cabinet. His wit is quick, and supple; he is practically the inventor of the French Colonial Department; he is a very consistently vigorous champion of French Colonial development, and in spite of all this he is very French. With all his pugnacity, or because of it, he likes music.

So he is a habitué of the Opera."

Vanity Fair, 9 February 1899

63
JEAN BAPTISE GUTH (1883-1921)
M. Théophile Delcassé
'French Foreign Affairs'
Signed and dated 98
Watercolour
12 x 6 ¾ inches
Provenance: A G Witherby;
The John Franks Collection
Illustrated: *Vanity Fair*, 9 February 1899, Men of the Day no 738, 'French Foreign Affairs'
Exhibited: 'In Vanity Fair', Stanford University, San Francisco, September-November 1980;
'Vanity Fair 1869-1914', Church Farm House Museum, Hendon, September-December 1983

CLOISTER (SIR CHARLES GARDEN DUFF) (1852-1914)
Lord Justice Williams

At the time of this portrait in Vanity Fair, Sir Roland Lomax Vaughan Williams (1838-1916) was serving as a Lord Justice of the Court of Appeal, a post he held from 1897 to 1914.

'A Rustic Judge'

"Roland Lomax Vaughan Williams, whose father was a Judge of the Court of Common Pleas, is sixty-one years old, a Westminster boy, a Christ Church man, a Lord Justice of Appeal, a very able fellow, and the most untidy of all Her Majesty's Judges. He lives hard by Earl's Court Station; and being no respecter of persons, it is said of him that he once carried a fender there from chambers under his arm. He is a rustic Judge, who is at home in the country; and even in the Strand, as he walks from the Courts, he is known by his badly-dressed person. But he is as clever as he is slovenly, and he owns a smile that is quite his own. His fault on the Bench is that his head is too big. He is a very strong Judge, but his brain sometimes thinks ahead of the Law; and, though he is seldom legally wrong, he is inclined to see farther than his brethren. He has in him, in fact, a streak of genius: and Genius does not always agree with Law. As a Counsel he was so untrammelled by tradition that he never even wagged a finger at the Bench; but he nodded his head until he earned the style of 'The Mandarin'. He has a blinking eye and a ponderous utterance; but he has not enemies: not even among present Westminsters – as they lately showed him when he gave them their athletic prizes. He was a distinct acquisition to the Bench, on which he succeeded Mr Justice Manisty; and, as the Lord Justice that he now is, he is strong, industrious, learned, and above the least suspicion of partiality.

No one could well call him an ornament of the Bench; but he is an exceedingly good Judge."

Vanity Fair, 2 March 1899

64
Cloister (Sir Charles Garden Duff) (1852-1914)
Lord Justice Williams
'A Rustic Judge'
Signed with initials
A letter to the artist is attached on reverse
Watercolour and bodycolour with pencil
13 ½ x 9 inches
Illustrated: *Vanity Fair*, 2 March 1899, Judges no 54,
'A Rustic Judge'

CLOISTER (SIR CHARLES GARDEN DUFF) (1852-1914)
Sir William George Granville Venables Vernon Harcourt, PC, MP, QC

Sir William Harcourt (1827-1904) was a Liberal politician who served as Home Secretary (1880 to 1885) and twice as Chancellor of the Exchequer, briefly in 1886 and from 1892 to 1895, under Prime Minister William Gladstone. Harcourt led the Liberal party as Leader of the Opposition from 1896 to 1898, before retiring from the party. At the time of his caricature by Cloister, he was a private member of parliament, though he continued to involve himself in government policy. Sir William Harcourt first appeared in *Vanity Fair* in 1870, drawn by Alfred Thompson.

'A Retired Leader'

"He is now a Politician of seventy-two; but there is as great difference between the old 'Historicus' and the new Ecclesiastic as there might be between the Squire of Malwood and the Bishop thereof. He is also the retired Leader of a (once) great Party: who in his retirement takes much interest in the position of the Church; and so may be imagined by the vain fancier as the denizen of some Cloister. But, though he is now retired, he is still the gentle Radical that he was. He knows all about everything better than any other; and he is still a reverent follower of the Shade of that Grand Old Man who once proved himself his better.

He is a merry fellow in his newest guise."

Vanity Fair, 11 May 1899

65
CLOISTER (SIR CHARLES GARDEN DUFF) (1852-1914)
Sir William George Granville Venables Vernon Harcourt, PC, MP, QC
'A Retired Leader'
Signed, inscribed
'You may think this sketch is rather silly
It's really meant for "Uncle Willie"
Around his waist he wears a robe
and swears his Leader is the "Pope"',
and dated 1899
Watercolour with pencil
13 ½ x 9 inches
Illustrated: *Vanity Fair*, 11 May 1899, Statesman no 707,
'A Retired Leader'

You may think this sketch is rather silly It's really meant for "Uncle Willie"
Around His waist He wears a rope And swears His Leader is the "Pope"

SPY (SIR LESLIE WARD) (1851-1922)
Ignace Jan Paderewski

At the time of his portrayal in *Vanity Fair*, Ignacy Paderewski (1860-1941) was a world renowned pianist and composer, perhaps best known for the composition 'Minuet in G'. A lifelong spokesman for Polish independence, Paderewski was appointed Prime Minister and Minister of Foreign Affairs of the newly independent Poland at the end of the First World War.

'Easy Execution'

"Nine-and-thirty years ago he became, in spite of himself, a Russian Pole in Podolia; and only three years later, though (or because) his circumstances were very unsympathetic, he played the piano. At twelve he went to Warsaw to learn harmony and counterpoint from Roguski; at eighteen he was a teacher, and a year or two later his talent urged him to virtue so strongly that he gave up everything to practice. After three hard years of study at Vienna he made his most successful début; and though he never appeared in England until he was thirty, his career was then assured as that of a great musician. His first appearance in Paris in 1889 encouraged him to come over to England; where he is now supposed to command a thousand guineas for a piece or two. He is a Commander of the Order of the Crown of Italy; but, for the rest, Music is his mistress and his honours are those of Music. For he is now both the first of living pianists and a really fine composer; whose great success has been achieved by earnest study and incessant practice helped by natural ability. He has also earned nearly £40,000 by a single tour.

In his own country he is the most popular of Poles; for his good, full heart has not been spoiled by success. He is also a patriotic enthusiast who spends money with unfailing ardour in the cause of Charity: so much so that when he had once emptied his pockets he said: 'I will go to America and fill them.' Socially he is a charming person, despite his uncut hair; whom women adore: some for his music; some because he is the fashion, and others for their own foolishness. He is an indefatigable worker and a Poet born: of whom it is scarce too much to say that he may be the re-incarnation of Chopin.

He must be heard before he is judged."

Vanity Fair, 28 December 1899

CLOISTER (SIR CHARLES GARDEN DUFF) (1852-1914)
Mr Arthur Yates

Born into a family of seed merchants in Lancashire, Arthur Yates (1841-1926) was sent to New Zealand at the age of 18 for his health. He opened a small seed shop in Auckland before settling in Sydney, Australia in 1888. In 1893, Yates launched a profitable range of packet seeds and two years later published a gardening book, *Yates' Gardening Guide for Australia and New Zealand: Hints for Amateurs*. By 1896 his business had become the largest of its kind in the colonies and he regularly travelled to England and Europe in search of quality seeds, whilst maintaining close ties with his father's business in Manchester.

'Arthur'

"Born nearly nine-and-fifty years ago, it has been said that the saddle was his cradle; and almost as soon as he could play at horses in the nursery he could ride them at a fence. At ten, indeed, he hunted a pack of harriers; and while still a boy he did the same by his father's staghounds in Hampshire. At nineteen he owned a bloodhorse in Playman; given him by that fine old sportsman who is now called Lord Brampton, yet is still better known as Sir Henry Hawkins. With his 'owner up' Playman won races, and his owner took to racing. Since then he has won an enormous number of steeplechases; for four years he was at the head of the gentlemen riders; he nearly won the Grand National on his own Harvester; and he has since trained that great winner of the same race, Mr. C. G. Duff's Cloister; who won the big steeplechase seven years ago in a walk, in what is still record time, and with a then record weight of twelve stone seven pounds. He now weighs sixteen stone, yet is he one of the best of trainers who owns the biggest steeplechase stable in the country. He once trained a winner for the Duke of Connaught; and his clients include most Officers who race. He is very fond of animals, his aviaries are full of rare birds, he keeps many deer, he is a capital shot, a good host, and a very popular fellow.

He is a gentleman whom his friends know as 'Arthur'."

Vanity Fair, 11 January 1900

67
CLOISTER (SIR CHARLES GARDEN DUFF) (1852-1914)
Mr Arthur Yates
'Arthur'
Signed
Watercolour and bodycolour
13 ½ x 9 ½ inches
Illustrated: *Vanity Fair*, 11 January 1900, Men of the Day no 770, 'Arthur'

SPY (SIR LESLIE WARD) (1851-1922)
Mr Arthur de Rothschild

A member of the prominent Rothschild banking family, Arthur de Rothschild (1851-1903) was the son of Nathaniel de Rothschild, a winemaker and founder of the Château Mouton Rothschild. Arthur de Rothschild was an enthusiastic art collector and philatelist. He also held a keen interest in yachting, and provided prize money for the America's Cup.

'Eros'

"He is very well known in Paris, and even more so at Monte Carlo. He owns a very beautiful yacht called the Eros, upon which he 'does' many parties very well. He is enormously rich; and he is quite partial to the Board of Green Cloth.

He is very fond of Art; and he is quite good-natured."

Vanity Fair, 2 August 1900

68
SPY (SIR LESLIE WARD) (1851-1922)
Mr Arthur de Rothschild
'Eros'
Signed
Inscribed with title and 'Baron Alphonse' on reverse
Watercolour with bodycolour on tinted paper
12 ¼ x 7 ½ inches
Provenance: A G Witherby; The John Franks Collection
Illustrated: *Vanity Fair*, 2 August 1900, Men of the Day no 786, 'Eros'

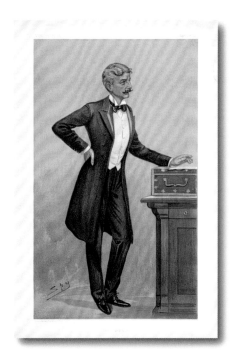

SPY (SIR LESLIE WARD) (1851-1922)
Mr George Wyndham, MP

Sir George Wyndham (1863-1913) served in the army as a young man before entering the House of Commons as MP for Dover in 1889, a seat he would hold until his death in 1913. Wyndham was a central figure in Souls, an aristocratic group formed in 1887 in reaction to the Prince of Wales's Marlborough House set. Also aspiring to be an author and artist, he published a number of works, such as *The Poems of Shakespeare* (1898), *Ronsard and La Pléiade* (1906) and *Essays in Romantic Literature*, published posthumously in 1919. In 1898 he was appointed as under-secretary at the War Office and in 1900, at the age of thirty-seven, was named Chief Secretary for Ireland.

'Dover and War'

"'Vonce round his vaist twice round a hearwig's,' said Mr. Punch in the early forties of a Statesman of the day. 'Agag' has many advantages. Well-born seven-and-thirty years ago, and well-married at twenty-four, he was sent to Eton (where they taught him the art of polite letter-writing); was forwarded to Sandhurst; served for three years in the Coldstream Guards and fitted himself for War by smelling powder at Saukim, became a Justice of the Peace for Cheshire and a Major of Yeomanry, went into Parliament for Dover, and has improved himself ever since. As Private Secretary to Mr. Arthur Balfour he combined the writing of official correspondence concerning the Plan of Campaign and the rest of it with the direction (in his spare moments) of the London, Chatham, and Dover Railway. In the one capacity he wrote letters that goaded the Bhoys to madness, being models of light-hearted yet perfectly correct literature; in the other Office he certainly did not impede the progress of any of the company's trains. Then he found apotheosis on the Front Bench of the House of Commons, where he gracefully reclines (sometimes with his boots on the table and his hands in his pockets) between Warrior Williams (on his left) and Jesse Collings (on his right). He is a Member of the Society of Souls; but as Under-Secretary for War he did much to save the bacon of the Government when Parliament met in February last, and it is beyond doubt that his manners and his appearance and his frock-coats have caught the ear of the House. He has indeed made a big reputation for himself; and as he has already learned a thing or two about the Army, and as, though he has caught the infection of the Official Optimist, he admits that the best of all possible Departments does need a spring cleaning, he is really full of promise, and pretty certain to remain the representative of Dover. For he is a very clever fellow who is quite full of possibilities.

He is not only praised of 'Tay Pay,' and admired of The Daily News; *but having 'arrived,' he may be depended upon to go far."*

Vanity Fair, 20 September 1900

69
SPY (SIR LESLIE WARD) (1851-1922)
Mr George Wyndham, MP
'Dover and War'
Watercolour and bodycolour with pencil
11 ¾ x 11 ¼ inches
Illustrated: *Vanity Fair*, 20 September 1900, Statesmen no 728, 'Dover and War'

SPY (SIR LESLIE WARD) (1851-1922)
Lord Raglan

Shortly before his portrait appeared in *Vanity Fair*, the Lord Raglan George Somerset had, in November 1900, been appointed Under-Secretary for War in Lord Salisbury's Conservative government. His grandfather, Lord FitzRoy Somerset, had served under the Duke of Wellington during the Napoleonic Wars, losing an arm at Waterloo in 1815. He was made Field Marshall of the British Armed Forces in the Crimea, where, in 1854, he was partly responsible for the ill-fated 'Charge of the Light Brigade'. George Somerset continued the military tradition of his family by joining the Grenadier Guards and seeing action in the Second Anglo-Afghan War, where he was decorated. In 1902, after serving as Under-Secretary for War, he was appointed Lieutenant Governor of the Isle of Man.

'Under-Secretary for War'

"Lord Fitzroy James Henry Somerset, eighth son of the fifth Duke of Beaufort, was the famous Field Marshal who Commanded the British Forces in the Crimea. He also won much glory with Wellington, lost an arm at Waterloo, and was created Baron Raglan of Raglan in Monmouthshire. He died at Sebastopol, and was succeeded by his eldest surviving son; who three-and-forty years ago became the father of George FitzRoy Henry Somerset: who is the third Baron and our new Under-Secretary of State for War. He is a sound Tory who learned Conservatism and easy, jovial manners as a Dry-bob at Eton: despite the fact that he was privileged to be a Page of Honour to Queen Victoria. He went to Sandhurst and joined the Grenadier Guards, was made a Captain, went over to the Monmouthshire Militia Engineers, is an Honorary Lieutenant-Colonel, has been Aide-de-Camp to a Governor of Bombay, and was Orderly Officer to General Sir R. Phayre in the Afghan War: when he earned a medal. Consequently he knows something of war, and may presently know something of the War Office. He owns eight hundred acres of Welsh land and Cefntilla Court: which was presented to his warlike grandfather by a grateful crowd of public subscribers. He likes soldiering, he is an excellent shot, he is full of energy, and he is a member of the Council of the Royal United Service Institution; where he is quite well known. He does not like frock coats, and he never wears a collar-stud; though two or three pipes may generally be found upon him.

He is a hearty good fellow, with brains; who can tell a glass of good port, and has been known to play bridge.

He is called 'Chaux'; but he does not like Salisbury Plain."

Vanity Fair, 14 February 1901

70
SPY (SIR LESLIE WARD) (1851-1922)
Lord Raglan
'Under-Secretary for War'
Signed
Watercolour with bodycolour and pencil
14 x 7 ½ inches
Illustrated: *Vanity Fair*, 14 February 1901, Statesmen no 732, 'Under-Secretary for War'

SIR LESLIE WARD, RP (1851-1922)
The Earl of Rosebery

As the fifth earl of Rosebery, a title he succeeded on the death of his grandfather in 1868, Archibald Primrose (1847-1929) served as Prime Minister of a Liberal government from 1894 to 1895. He had become Prime Minister following the retirement of William Ewart Gladstone, having served under Gladstone as Foreign Secretary in 1886 and again between 1892 and 1894. Following the defeat of the Liberal Party in June 1895, Rosebery remained as Liberal leader until his resignation and subsequent retirement from politics in October 1896.

At the time of his appearance in *Vanity Fair*, though he was officially politically inactive, Rosebery had emerged as the leader of the 'Liberal Imperialists' faction of the party, vocally supporting the Boer War and opposing Irish Home Rule.

'Little Bo-Peep'

"The first Charles found a Primrose and made him Clerk of his Privy Council; 'whereupon Primrose honourably stood by his Master through the Civil Wars, and the Primroses became a Family.' So much was said here of his origin just a quarter of a century ago; when he was less than thirty years of age, had come of reputable forbears, and had done with Eton and the House. At one-and-twenty he addressed the House of Lords upon horses; and his faith is still in the noble animal. He fills all sorts of Offices, from the Leadership of an absent Party to a Trusteeship of the Imperial Institute, and he sometimes manages to make quite a sensation. He has filled even bigger Offices, such as that of the Sovereign's Prime Minister and the Lord Rectorship of Glasgow University; but he has never yet redeemed his early promise. For just as he is at this moment a Leader of no Party, so has he been a Statesman full of possibilities but without that balance which is needed for really great success. Sometimes, indeed, he has been roundly accused of playing to the gallery; yet has he always been a persona grata with Personages. He is a clever fellow who is often called able; but with all his cleverness, his brilliance, and his wit he reminds one of a man with ten talents who does nothing with them. He has won two Derbys running, and he is popular on the Turf; yet in the great Affairs of the Empire he seems to let his chances – and they have been many – slip. He is supposed to know all about Foreign Affairs; and twice he has been their Secretary of State; but, like a brilliant meteor, he has left no mark upon the shifting sands of time. He still has a future before him, for he is but three-and-fifty. Will he ever overtake it?

He is a fine orator and a warm critic. He has compiled two little books, and he has enemies."

Vanity Fair, 14 March 1901

71
Sir Leslie Ward, RP (1851-1922)
The Earl of Rosebery
'Little Bo-Peep'
Signed
Watercolour and bodycolour
11 x 7 inches
Illustrated: *Vanity Fair*, 14 March 1901, Statesmen no 734,
'Little Bo-Peep'

SPY (SIR LESLIE WARD) (1851-1922)
Mr Charles Santley

Sir Charles Santley (1834-1922) was an opera singer who began his career with the Liverpool Philharmonic Society on his fifteenth birthday, before travelling to study in Milan. In 1857, having performed in Milan and Pavia, he returned to England. Until his final operatic performance in 1876, he sang in operas across the country, rising to fame for his roles in productions of *The Marriage of Figaro, Les Huguenots* and *Faust*. From 1876 he only sang in concert, such as at the opening of the Albert Hall in 1871, the same year he was awarded the gold medal of the Royal Philharmonic Society. In 1907 he became the first singer ever to be knighted. He was referred to by George Bernard Shaw as 'the best baritone singer with whom the London public is familiar'.

'Student and Singer'

"Sixty eight years ago he was born in Liverpool with vocal chords that have since sung him into the front flight of baritones. He worked hard both in England and in Italy until his first public appearance in London in 1857; and he has worked hard ever since. After two years he made a success in the opera 'Dinorah' so great that it led him in triumph to Australia and to the Cape. Then 'Lurline' assured him of pre-eminence, and he has operatically kept himself pre-eminent in most of the capitals of Europe. He can raise his voice from the basso profundo to a pure tenore robusto, while its quality is unrivalled; and, apart from his art and his talent, he deserves all the success that he has achieved. For he is a kindly fellow, who has often gone out of his way to encourage young singers. He was once guilty of a book; but he has nothing of the shoddy school about him.

He can still give 'To Anthea' with a fervour that the heartiest of troubadours might envy."

Vanity Fair, 27 February 1902

72
Spy (Sir Leslie Ward) (1851-1922)
Mr Charles Santley
'Student and Singer'
Signed
Watercolour with bodycolour and pencil on tinted paper
11 ½ x 8 inches
Provenance: A G Witherby;
Stanley Jackson; The John Franks Collection
Illustrated: *Vanity Fair*, 27 February 1902, Men of the Day no 835,
'Student and Singer'

SPY (SIR LESLIE WARD) (1851-1922)
John Gordon Swift MacNeill, KC, MP

Born in Dublin, John Gordon Swift McNeill (1849-1926) practised law as a young man, being called to the Irish bar in 1876 and elected professor of constitutional and criminal law at the King's Inns, Dublin in 1882. He was an advocate of Irish Home Rule and published propagandistic works such as *The Irish Parliament: What it Was, and What it Did* (1885). From 1887 to 1918, he sat as MP for South Donegal before retiring from parliament.

'South Donegal'

"He is a parson's son of three-and-fifty who ought to know better; but if he does not always behave as an Irish gentleman should, he is an Irish barrister who claims relationship with the late Dean Swift. He has taken classical honours at Trinity College, Dublin, and at Christ Church, Oxford, and he obstructs legislation on behalf of South Donegal in the unfortunate House of Commons while he professes Constitutional and Criminal Law in King's Inns. He is an extreme Home Ruler who, although he was believed to be attached to the Tim Healyite faction, is at home in the zareba of John Redmond without ever being antagonistic to Mr. Dillon. He has probably been called to order by the Speaker more often than any other Irishman; for he is politically full of insignificant sound and fury. He is also a pro-Boer who yet had friends in the House until Monday last: when by applauding the painful news of a national disaster he succeeded in overstepping the limits of bad taste."

Vanity Fair, 13 March 1902

73
SPY (SIR LESLIE WARD) (1851-1922)
John Gordon Swift MacNeill, KC, MP
'South Donegal'
Signed
Watercolour and bodycolour with pencil on tinted paper
12 x 7 inches
Illustrated: *Vanity Fair*, 13 March 1902, Statesmen no 748,
'South Donegal'

SPY (SIR LESLIE WARD) (1851-1922)
The Reverend Henry Montagu Villiers, MA

Henry Montagu Villiers (1837-1908) held the office of Prebendary of St Paul's Cathedral and later served as the Vicar of St Paul's Church, Knightsbridge.

'St Paul's Knightsbridge'

"The Vicar of St Paul's, Knightsbridge, is what the ladies of his fashionable congregation call a 'dear creature'; and he really is a good fellow, who has preached many excellent sermons that are better written than they are delivered, since he left the House two-and-forty years ago. He is not very beautiful to look at, but there is no better persuader of money out of ladies' pockets to charitable ends; so that he has been called a splendid beggar. He has an excellent living, he fills a big church, he has inherited money, and, though he is a very High-Churchman, he has been seen drinking tea in an aerated bread shop.

He is a big man with two big families."

Vanity Fair, 21 August 1902

74
SPY (SIR LESLIE WARD) (1851-1922)
The Reverend Henry Montagu Villiers, MA
'St Paul's Knightsbridge'
Signed
Watercolour and bodycolour with pencil
12 x 7 ½ inches
Illustrated: *Vanity Fair*, 21 August 1902, Men of the Day no 847,
'St Paul's Knightsbridge'

SPY (SIR LESLIE WARD) (1851-1922)
Jan Kubelik

Jan Kubelik (1880-1940) was a Czech violinist who toured the world as a soloist from 1898. After debuting in Vienna, he first played in London in 1900 at a Hans Richter concert, before touring the USA in 1901. He returned to London later the same year with the Royal Philharmonic Society and was award the society's Gold Medal in 1902. Later that year, he was credited with bringing the Czech Philharmonic Orchestra to London through his own financial assistance.

'Kubelik'

"He was only born, in Michle, three-and-twenty years ago, yet he has drawn sweeter strains from the strings of a violin than any other player of our time. His father was a market gardener in Bohemia; but the son was sent to practise at the Prague Conservatoire. At eighteen he began to give recitals which drew the world; he has since travelled all over Europe, conquering each capital in turn, and through America; earning acclamation, and winning Orders and Distinctions everywhere. England loves him and America runs after him; so that he is reputed to have made several fortunes. This is because there is genius in him; which is possibly aided by a striking personality. To hear him play is a revelation; to watch his modest demeanour when he finishes amid applause that would swell most heads is another: for his Art is his mistress and he is not to be easily spoiled.

He is a quiet, amiable, unassuming fellow, who is promised in marriage to a charming lady."

Vanity Fair, 7 May 1903

75
Spy (Sir Leslie Ward) (1851-1922)
Jan Kubelik
'Kubelik'
Signed
Watercolour and bodycolour on tinted paper
12 ½ x 7 ¾ inches
Illustrated: *Vanity Fair*, 7 May 1903, Men of the Day no 877, 'Kubelik'

SPY (SIR LESLIE WARD) (1851-1922)
The Earl of Shrewsbury and Talbot

When only seventeen years old, Major Charles Chetwynd-Talbot (1860-1921) inherited the titles of the 20th Earl of Shrewsbury, 20th Earl of Waterford and 5th Earl of Talbot. Passionate about equestrian sports, he developed an interest in horse-drawn transport and, in London in 1888, founded the Shrewsbury and Talbot Cab and Noiseless Tyre Company; this would grow to 210 cabs and 365 horses. Following his separation from his wife in 1896, she remained at Alton Towers, Staffordshire, while he went to live at Ingestre Hall, in the same county. There, in 1903, he founded the Talbot car company in order to import the French Clément car into Britain, which began in 1905. Domestically designed Talbot cars followed from 1906.

'Cabs'

"At the age of seventeen, Charles Henry John Chetwynd-Talbot, Earl of Shrewsbury and Talbot, succeeded his father as twentieth Earl six-and-twenty years ago. Nevertheless, he can trace his lineage behind the Norman Conquest, Richard de Talbot being mentioned in Domesday Book; and he is the premier Earl of England, as well as Hereditary Great Seneschal (Lord High Steward) of Ireland, and various other things. The history of his eminent House fills more than six pages of Burke, and himself is a man who never lets his pleasures interfere with his work: which he began at Eton. Yet he is so fond of coaching that for several seasons he ran the Greyhound coach from Buxton to his own Alton Towers. He is also one of the keenest of motor drivers, and chairman of a big motor manufactory; while he is a playing member of the chief polo clubs, and quite a keen man to hounds. He is, in fact, a first-rate all-round sportsman, of whom it has been said that his hobby is cabs. He claims to have had his ups and downs in life, but he has two children to whom he is devoted, his son and he being more like brothers than anything else. He shoots all the autumn, he hunts all the winter, he plays polo all the summer, and he motors all the year; yet he never lets any of these amusements interfere with the management of his collieries, estates, and other businesses. With the 'S. T.' hansoms he showed what rubber tyres could do in London, and then did the same turn to Paris, Brussels, and Milan. Now he goes in for motors and pneumatics, and has started a new factory for making French cars by English workmen at Notting Hill; which has put out five hundred motors in its first year.

He is a kindly, good-tempered fellow with brains; who has friends."

Vanity Fair, 30 July 1903

76
Spy (Sir Leslie Ward) (1851-1922)
The Earl of Shrewsbury and Talbot
'Cabs'
Signed
Watercolour and bodycolour
12 ¼ x 8 ¼ inches
Illustrated: *Vanity Fair*, 30 July 1903, Statesmen no 758, 'Cabs'

Spy (Sir Leslie Ward) (1851-1922)
Sir Alexander Campbell Mackenzie, Mus Doc, LLD, DCL

Sir Alexander Mackenzie (1847-1935) was a composer and conductor, who also trained as a violinist. Born in Edinburgh, he moved to London in 1862 and entered the Royal Academy of Music. He returned to Edinburgh following the completion of his studies in 1865 and remained there until 1881, when he moved to Florence for the sake of his health. He returned to London in 1887 to become Principal of the Royal Academy of Music, a position he held until his retirement in 1924. From 1892 to 1899 Mackenzie was conductor of the Philharmonic Society's concerts, and he was knighted in 1895.

'R.A.M.'

"Born in 1847, he inherited musical ability from his father, Alexander Mackenzie, of the Theatre Royal, Edinburgh, who was an excellent violinist. From Edinburgh he was sent to Schwarzburg-Sondershausen, a town then noted for the way in which it fostered the art of modern music. It fostered Mackenzie's so well that at the age of thirteen he was a violinist in the Ducal Orchestra; and he still thanks those who drilled him in the rudiments of music for much that he has since achieved. From Germany he came to town as a pupil under Sainton at the Royal Academy of Music, of which he has now been Principal for nearly seventeen years. He won the King's Scholarship, he learned to play upon the piano, he worked very hard and became famous as a player on the violin with such artists as Joachim, Norman-Neruda, Wilhelmj, and Strauss. Then Von Bulow and Manns encouraged him to compose. He did so, and went to Florence to write 'The Bride', 'Jason', and other works. Since then he has been guilty of 'The Troubadour', opera, ' A Jubilee Ode', cantata, and 'La Belle Dame Sans Merci', as well as many other works of more or less weight, up to a Savoy opera, 'His Majesty', and 'The Coronation March', which he dedicated to his King. He has also clapped the Man in the Street on his back with his 'Britannia', overture, and 'London Day by Day'. He is now a Knight at the top of the musical tree, to whom a large, personally conducted band of pupils is devoted; while he has been given so many degrees by different Universities that he is one of the most 'doctored' men in London.

More personally, he is a Scotchman with a very real sense of humour, who, having left his native country, successfully dared to go back there on the most unremunerative errand − that of composing high-class music; while he can claim the distinction of having had some of his works played more than once − an almost incredible honour for a Britisher. Altogether he is a great musician and a fine leader whose orchestras are very pleased with his conduct.

He is a genial fellow and a very hard worker; so earnest that after a big performance there is very little left in him."

Vanity Fair, 14 January 1904

77
Spy (Sir Leslie Ward) (1851-1922)
Sir Alexander Campbell Mackenzie, Mus Doc, LLD, DCL
'R.A.M.'
Signed
Inscribed with title below mount
Watercolour with bodycolour and pencil on tinted paper
13 ½ x 7 ¼ inches
Illustrated: *Vanity Fair,* 14 January 1904, Men of the Day no 905, 'R.A.M'

'A Great Marrier'

SPY (SIR LESLIE WARD) (1851-1922)
The Reverend Edgar Sheppard, DD, CVO

At the time of his appearance in *Vanity Fair*, the Reverend Edgar Sheppard (1845-1921) was Honorary Chaplain to King Edward VII and Deputy Clerk of the Closet. From 1907 until his death in 1921, he was Canon of Windsor.

'A Great Marrier'

"The Sub-Dean of the Chapels Royal and Confessor of the Household at St James's Palace became the son of a Professor of Psychology at King's College nine-and-fifty years ago. Educated at home and at St. John's, Oxford (where he was a noted singer) he began clerical life as Curate of Marlow, and later, at Hornsey under Canon Harvey; but being full of music as well as of other graces, he presently improved himself into a Minor Canon of St. George's, Windsor; and naturally became Priest-in-Ordinary to Queen Victoria. He makes no mistakes, so that he is now a very important person, by whom it is a fashionable privilege to be married. He is Clerk of the Closet, Sub-Almoner and Chaplain-in-Ordinary to his King; and he was also Chaplain to the Duke of Cambridge. Further, he is Chaplain of the Order of St. John of Jerusalem, and, of course, also to the Royal Society of Musicians. For he owes a good deal to his musical attainments, and to him is greatly due the excellence of the Choir of the Chapel Royal. He has a strong yet melodious voice, and though he is not a great preacher, his sermons are sensible and moderate, and he has the rare faculty of knowing when to leave off. His kindness to those in need, sorrow, sickness, or any other adversity, from the highest to the lowest, is unbounded; so that he is a general favourite, as well as the author of two popular books, 'Memorials of St. James's Palace', and 'The Old Royal Palace of Whitehall'.

Altogether, he is become so indispensable that it is next to impossible for anyone to be born, married, or buried without his assistance."

Vanity Fair, 24 March 1904

78
Spy (Sir Leslie Ward) (1851-1922)
The Reverend Edgar Sheppard, DD, CVO
'A Great Marrier'
Signed
Inscribed with title on reverse
Watercolour and bodycolour with pencil
12 ½ x 8 inches
Illustrated: *Vanity Fair*, 24 March 1904, Men of The Day no 911, 'A Great Marrier'

79
Spy (Sir Leslie Ward) (1851-1922)
Sir Hiram Stevens Maxim
'In The Clouds'
Signed
Watercolour and bodycolour on tinted paper
13 x 9 inches
Provenance: A G Witherby; The John Franks Collection
Illustrated: *Vanity Fair*, 15 December 1904, Men of the Day
no 943, 'In The Clouds'
Exhibited: '*Vanity Fair* 1869-1914', Church Farm House Museum,
Hendon, September-December 1983

SPY (SIR LESLIE WARD) (1851-1922)
Sir Hiram Stevens Maxim

Sir Hiram Maxim (1840-1916) was an American engineer and inventor who found fame as the creator of the Maxim Gun, the world's first recoil-operated automatic machine gun. Born in Maine, USA, he rose to the position of chief engineer at the United States Electric Lighting Company. In this role, he was involved in installing the first electric lights in a New York City building and was involved in numerous patent disputes with Thomas Edison over the invention of the lightbulb. In 1881, he moved to the London offices of the United States Electric Lighting Company and by 1884 had begun to focus on weaponry, founding the Maxim Gun Company that year. His Maxim Gun was adopted in the British army in 1889 and in the Royal Navy in 1892. Maxim became a naturalised British citizen in 1900 and was knighted the following year.

'In The Clouds'

"Fifty four years ago an apprentice entered a wheelwright's shop. To do this he travelled from his home in Sangerville, Piscatakui County, to East Corinth Village. Both these centres of progress are in Maine, U.S.A. The apprentice was by birth a Maxim, and by paternal selection a Hiram. The latter name is not uncommon in the vicinity.

From East Corinth Hiram moved to Abbot and began to invent. The first effort was a tricycle, the second a mouse-trap, the third a blackboard. Then came the Civil War, the end of which terrible struggle found Hiram building gas engines. Peace brought swelling trade to his country and the first electric lighting company to Hiram. While in charge of it he was defrauded of a monopoly of the world by the publication of an indiscreet article. He still regrets the fact.

He first thought of the Maxim gun by receiving a jar on the shoulder at the firing of an old rifle. It seemed a pity that the kick should be wasted. Therefore he put the recoil to work in automatic loading and firing at the rate of a thousand shots a minute. The name of the inventor has gathered popularity thereby amongst all people save a few barbarians such as the Matabele, Soudanese, and Somalis, where there is an odd prejudice against him. But your true barbarian is ever a foe to progress.

Observing that a goose can fly, Hiram, now become Sir Hiram and a British subject, determined to imitate it. This little idea cost him £30,000. When the machine did fly it made the mistake of coming down. Then it smashed. But though his body still remains on terra-firma the soul of this aerial Tom Bowling is ever in the clouds. He has found that the flying machine which twirls at the end of a rope at sixpence a ride pays better than unsupported flight. Therein does he show his wisdom. It is rare that common sense walks hand in hand with invention.

He has written a book about Monte Carlo, where Sir Hiram's maxims are ever popular. He rises early and works late. He believes in an eight hours day; that is eight hours before lunch, and eight hours after. He has made a hobby of the patent laws. He is a strong anti-clerical but has a Christian spirit – patents always excepted."

Vanity Fair, 15 December 1904

80
SPY (SIR LESLIE WARD) (1851-1922)
Mr Egerton Castle
**'He insists that his pen is mightier
than his sword'**
Signed
Watercolour and bodycolour
14 x 8 inches
Illustrated: *Vanity Fair*, 9 March 1905, Men of the Day
no 954, 'He insists his pen is mightier than his sword'

SPY (SIR LESLIE WARD) (1851-1922)
Mr Egerton Castle

Born into a wealthy publishing family, Egerton Castle was an author and swordsman, and was a leading figure in the revival of the art of historical fencing. In 1885, he wrote *Schools and Masters of Fencing: From the Middle Ages to the Eighteenth Century*, the standard reference on the sport, and captained the British epeé and sabre teams at the 1908 Olympic Games. He also found fame as writer of fiction, co-authoring several novels with his wife, Agnes. A number of these novels, including *The Pride of Jennico* (1897), *Rose of the World* (1905) and *The Bath Comedy* (1900), were later adapted into silent films.

'He insists that his pen is mightier than his sword'

"Mr Egerton Castle hides a kindly nature beneath a bellicose expression. His figure is one emphatic protest against the sombre utilitarianism of twentieth century clothes. A neat rapier would be something; but even that comfort is denied to him in modern walking dress. His method of fence is as graceful and romantic as the construction of his novels. He says that his pen is mightier than his sword; as a matter of perfection, there is little to choose between them.

In Mr. Egerton Castle, indeed, the play of the sword and the work of the pen have a definite relation. It was his youthful enthusiasm for killing his neighbour like a gentleman instead of clubbing him like a footpad which led him to write his first book - a history of the sword as the 'arbiter of honourable difficulties'. It may seem a long cry from 'Schools and Masters of Fence' to such books as 'Young April', 'The Secret Orchard', or 'Incomparable Bellairs'; yet it was the first-mentioned work, published nearly twenty years ago, that started him on the path of romantic literature.

His early youth was spent on the Continent. It was from a house in the Champs Elysées that his first impressions of life were gained; and it was under the care of Parisian professors that he made acquaintance with literature, romantic and otherwise. Nevertheless, do not mistake him for a foreigner. It will be unwise; also he has not a drop of blood in his veins that is anything but the best Anglo-Saxon. At sixteen he came to England, and fell upon learning with avidity. Glasgow University was followed by King's College (London), Trinity (Cambridge), the Inner Temple, Sandhurst, and Chatham; he became, in turns, student of History, Law, and Natural Science; and lastly soldier. It was no bad training for a novelist. He left the army to marry the charming Irish girl who was destined to become his literary as well as matrimonial partner.

Mr. Egerton Castle drifted slowly into a very busy life of letters. At first he aimed his free-lance at journalism, eventually joining the staff of the old Saturday Review. *He was a regular contributor until 1894, when that paper first changed hands. Much of his time was also expended on the* Liverpool Mercury, *which had been founded, a century ago, by his grandfather, Egerton Smith, the philanthropist, to whom Liverpool has erected a statue. Chairman of this newspaper company, he obtained an intimate acquaintance with the business side of journalism; and, quite recently, he had an important share in engineering the amalgamation of this paper into the* Liverpool Daily Post, Mercury and Echo.

Mr. Egerton Castle is a devout Imperialist. As a Vice-President of the Navy League, of which body he was one of the earliest members, he directs a critical eye upon all matters of Imperial defence. He dreams of the day when the peoples of the United States and the Old Country shall be gathered together in peace for the promotion of benefits to civilisation other than the formation of Trusts and subsidies to the Cunard Company. That he takes himself seriously is his single weakness; it is a failing not uncommon to genius."

Vanity Fair, 9 March 1905

SPY (SIR LESLIE WARD) (1851-1922)
Robert Henry Bullock-Marsham

At the time of his caricature in *Vanity Fair* in 1905, Robert Henry Bullock Marsham (1833-1913) was a magistrate at Bow Street Magistrates Court in London. In his youth, Marsham was a talented cricketer. He was selected to play for the Gentlemen against the Players at Lord's in 1859 and in 1860, featured for the MCC against Surrey at Lord's in July 1859 and was selected to play for England against Kent at Canterbury in 1860. His obituary appeared in the *Wisden Almanack* in 1913.

'Bow Street'

"Bob Marsham is a son of the some time Warden of Merton, for fifty-four years the most popular head of any Oxford college. He was born in 1833, when crime was less scientific and its punishment more brutal than at Bow Street to-day. He was educated at home by a private tutor, afterwards entering at Merton. His efforts to obtain honours in the mathematical schools did not prevent him from finding a place in the University eleven. He was chosen for the Gentlemen in their match against the Players at Lord's, his brother, C. D. Marsham, who was without doubt one of the best amateur bowlers of his time, being in the same team. At four-and-twenty he began to eat his dinners at the Inner Temple.

In 1860 Robert Bullock-Marsham was called to the Bar, and joined the South Eastern Circuit. He distinguished himself by acute discernment and sound unemotional judgment. He was never a sentimentalist to the jury, nor a humorist with the witness; but he did his work in a plain straightforward manner that won him cases. He was appointed Magistrate at Greenwich and Woolwich in 1879. Eighteen years later he was transferred to Westminster, and from that Court in 1809 he went to Bow Street, where he now shares the magisterial duties with Sir Albert de Rutzen and Mr. E. N. F. Fenwick.

His conduct on the Bench is noteworthy for the leniency with which he deals with many of the offenders who come before him. Young men and women who have strayed from the path of honesty have received at his hands an opportunity to reform, and his kindly words of warning and advice have often had a far greater effect in checking a criminal career than would a heavy sentence. He never displays the least sign of anger, and he favours no one. To the chagrin of many of the eminent counsel who sometimes appear before him, he has made it an inflexible rule to take each case in turn as it appears on his list, and in that way a prisoner is often spared the additional punishment of having to wait for trial till late in the day while the magistrate listens to a long legal argument.

The most trivial offence receives as much of his attention as the most heinous crime known to the law. He is an especial friend to the poor of his district, and is a patient listener to their tales of woe. He does not issue summonses indiscriminately, and often brings about an amicable settlement of a domestic quarrel by a kindly lecture to the person applying to him for redress, and by sending the warrant officer with a message to the person concerning whom complaint is made.

He has read the Riot Act in Trafalgar Square. He may often be seen at Lord's. His friends have nothing but kindly words to say about him."

Vanity Fair, 12 October 1905

81
Spy (Sir Leslie Ward) (1851-1922)
Robert Henry Bullock-Marsham
'Bow Street'
Signed
Inscribed 'Mr Bullock-Marsham' on reverse
Watercolour and bodycolour on tinted paper
13 x 8 inches
Provenance: A G Witherby;
The John Franks Collection
Illustrated: *Vanity Fair*, 12 October 1905, Men of the Day no 985, 'Bow Street'
Literature: Morris L Cohen, *The Bench and Bar, Great Legal Caricatures from 'Vanity Fair' by Spy*, New Haven, CT: Hugh Lauter Levin Associates, 1997, page 100
Exhibited: 'Vanity Fair 1869-1914', Church Farm House Museum, Hendon, September-December 1983

SPY (SIR LESLIE WARD) (1851-1922)
The Dean of Westminster

Joseph Armitage Robinson (1858-1933) was one of the leading Anglican clerics and theological scholars of the late nineteenth and early twentieth centuries. He was educated at Cambridge, and, as a fellow of Christ's College, taught and researched, while also taking up various positions, including that of domestic chaplain to J B Lightfoot, the Bishop of Durham and probably the leading European scholar of patristics (1883-84). His positions at Cambridge included Dean of Christ's College (1884-90) and Norrisian Professor of Divinity (1893-99). In 1891, he became editor of the first of a new series of Cambridge 'Texts and Studies', and was a key contributor to later numbers. As early as 1894, his impact on international scholarship was marked by honorary degrees from Göttingen and Halle universities.

In 1899, Robinson moved to London to become Rector of St Margaret's Westminster (1899-1900) and then Dean of Westminster (1902-11), the role in which Spy here presents him. The cathedral chapter sometimes considered his actions autocratic, and so it sought, unsuccessfully, to limit his powers. While at Westminster, he continued to publish, and distinguished himself as both a theologian and a historian. Especially important was his landmark commentary of St Paul's Epistle to the Ephesians (1908). In 1911, Robinson became Dean of Wells, in Somerset (which was already familiar to him as he had held the prebend of Compton Bishop during the late 1890s). Wells Cathedral stimulated his antiquarian interests, and the county of Somerset inspired further publications. During the 1920s, he became an active participant in the five Malines Conversations, which explored the possibilities of reunion between the Roman Catholic Church and the Church of England.

'An Erudite Dean'

"Dr. J. Armitage Robinson was born at Keynsham Vicarage, in Somerset, on January 9, 1858, being the third son of the Rev. George Robinson, who, removing to Liverpool later on, took his place as one of the leading evangelical clergymen in that city. His son, Armitage, went up from Liverpool College to Christ's College, Cambridge, where in 1881 he took a distinguished degree as fourth classic and winner of one of the Chancellor's Medals. He was elected Fellow of his College; but served his apprenticeship in Holy Orders as domestic chaplain to Bishop Lightfoot.

Recalled from Bishop Auckland to Cambridge in 1884, in order to become Dean of his College, he threw himself into the life of the University, where he spent the next fifteen years, for the last six of which he occupied the chair of the Norrisian Professor of Divinity. While thus engaged, he acquired a European reputation for his knowledge of early Christian literature. He also started and edited the Cambridge series of 'Texts and Studies', he himself publishing various works, the very titles of which show that they are caviare to the multitude. This devotion to study was balanced by preaching and other essays in practical divinity. He was for four years Vicar of All Saints', Cambridge; so that his appointment by Lord Salisbury in 1899 to a Canonry at Westminster with the Rectory of St. Margaret's was recognised as a fitting sequel to his career at Cambridge.

Three years later King Edward VII acceded to the Throne, and then it was found that in the Chapter of the Collegiate Church of St. Peter's, Westminster, Dr. Robinson was the one who had thoroughly mastered the ritual and traditions of the Coronation Service. Accordingly, when Dean Bradley had resigned at the following Michaelmas, it caused no surprise to hear that the King had nominated Dr. Robinson as his successor. Deans of Westminster have in times past generally been numbered among the octogenarians, and to appoint a Dean at the comparatively youthful age of forty-four was a rather unusual experiment. It has been justified.

Dr. Robinson's learning and scholarship befit a decanal stall; his appreciation of the history of the past with his sound artistic taste make him a trustworthy guardian of the most beautiful and famous of our national sanctuaries; while the dignity of his presence, enhanced by the ribbon of the Bath, lends an ornament to its services.

In appearance he is a thorough ecclesiastic, of a type which reminds me of the Church dignitaries of the early sixteenth century. A good raconteur, and possessed of a wit which is at times almost caustic, but always good-natured, he is an acquisition to the dinner table when he will dine out – for he has to some extent the student's tendency to become a recluse.

In ecclesiastical politics, the Dean of Westminster is hard to label. Born and bred in a strict evangelical family, broadened by critical studies at the University, with a natural inclination for ritual, and made a High Churchman by a deep realisation of the meaning of 'the Church', Dr. Robinson has sympathies with all the Church parties, and strenuously holds aloof from party warfare. His preaching, which is evangelic and simple, though scholarly, draws large congregations; and his Advent lectures, in which he applies his remarkable powers of lucid exposition to the unravelling of modern difficulties, have become a feature of the Abbey's yearly course. The Deanery reflects the character of the Dean. There is no Mrs. Robinson; and the place of a family is taken by a few young graduates, studying theology. A severe simplicity in its decorations, characterised by excellent taste, serves to keep the ancient 'Place' of the Abbots of Westminster in due harmony with their Church of Westminster and the considerable remains of its monastic surroundings."

Vanity Fair, 14 December 1905

82
Spy (Sir Leslie Ward) (1851-1922)
The Dean of Westminster
'An Erudite Dean'
Signed
Watercolour with bodycolour and pencil on tinted paper
14 ½ x 10 ½ inches
Illustrated: *Vanity Fair*, 14 December 1905, Men of the Day no 993, 'An Erudite Dean'

SPY (SIR LESLIE WARD) (1851-1922)
Mr Albert Brassey

At the time of his appearance in *Vanity Fair*, Albert Brassey (1844-1918) was the Conservative MP for Banbury, a seat he had held since 1895. Brassey spent much of his career in the army, serving as a lieutenant in the 14th Hussars and a colonel in the Queen's Own Oxfordshire Hussars, before servings as High Sheriff of Oxfordshire in 1878. A keen rower as a youth, he was part of Oxford teams that won the Grand Challenge Cup, Ladies' Challenge Plate and Visitors' Challenge Cup at the Henley Regatta.

'The Master of the Heythrop'

"Mr Albert Brassey is Master of the celebrated Heythrop Pack, the servants of which Hunt still sport the Beaufort green plush in compliment to the days when Badminton and Heythrop were closely associated. It is a long reign which connects Mr. Brassey with the Heythrop Hounds – commencing, indeed, in 1873 – and public opinion has bestowed upon him the title of 'Albert the Good' in recognition of a well-spent life and a strenuous nature, which enables him at the end of three score years both to work and play hard. A man of order, all things with him are orderly, and it may easily be supposed that his nature revolts against the haphazard modes of modern life.

He was educated at Eton and University College, Oxford, and rowed in the Eton eight in 1862. Later he joined the 14th Hussars, and while quartered at Cahir in 1870 hunted the Regimental Harriers. About this time he fell a victim to the most pleasing of all maladies that affect the heart, and married the eldest daughter of Lord Clanmorris.

Mr. Brassey is a member of the Four-in-Hand and Coaching Clubs, and his bays form a spanking team. He took a fair dose of Parliament, and held his seat in the Conservative interest for ten years. He never caught the Speaker's eye, but was beloved by the Whips for his regular attendance. He has the right while in town to breakfast at the Oxford and Cambridge, lunch at the Army and Navy, have tea at the Naval and Military, dine at the Carlton, and sup at the Cavalry; and, if none of these suit his palate, he can retire to his own well-regulated establishment in Berkeley Square. That he is a sportsman none has ever gainsaid, and upon his own land and midst the lovely surroundings of his stately home at Heythrop he is recognised as a just and generous landlord, and a bountiful donor to philanthropic schemes.

He sees as much of a fox-hunt as most of them, and his good common sense and prudence usually find him well placed at the finish. The kindly manner in which the youthful Oxonian has ever been welcomed with the Heythrop still lives in the memory of a host of full-grown sportsmen who had their first experience of the gentle art of falling with his hounds. Rebuke when deserved is courteously administered, and is reasonably effective, despite the absence of that loud-tongued abuse in which some Masters so greatly delight."

Vanity Fair, 15 March 1906

83
Spy (Sir Leslie Ward) (1851-1922)
Mr Albert Brassey
'The Master of the Heythrop'
Signed
Inscribed 'Brassey' on reverse
Watercolour and bodycolour on tinted paper
12 x 8 inches
Illustrated: *Vanity Fair*, 15 March 1906, Men of the Day no 1006, 'The Master of The Heythrop'

84
Spy (Sir Leslie Ward) (1851-1922)
Mr Henry J Wood
'Queen's Hall'
Signed and inscribed with title
Dated 1907 on reverse
Watercolour and bodycolour
18 x 14 ½ inches
Illustrated: *Vanity Fair*, 17 April 1907,
Men of the Day no 1062,
'Queen's Hall'

Spy (Sir Leslie Ward) (1851-1922)
Mr Henry J Wood

Sir Henry Wood (1869-1944), was a famed musician and conductor. In 1895 he inaugurated the Queen's Hall promenade concerts remaining in charge until 1940. The Henry Wood Promenade Concerts have been held at the Albert Hall from 1941 until the present day.

'Queen's Hall'

"One reads in 'Who's Who,' with a certain shock, these words: 'WOOD, Henry J., musician.' It is the 'musician' that shakes one's spirit, for though there can be no doubt that Mr. Wood is really a musician, nine hundred and ninety-nine persons out of a thousand would at first blush, as it were, speak of him rather as a conductor. In point of fact Mr. Wood appears to have conducted pretty well everything that is capable of being conducted, with the single exception of a revival meeting. He has figured as the conductor of the Rousbey Opera Company (1889), the Marie Roze Concert Tour (1890), the Carl Rosa Opera Company (1891), the Leslie Crotty and Georgina Burns Opera Company (1892) Signor Lago's Italian Opera Season (1893), the Farewell Concert Tour of Marie Roze (1894), and so on and so forth till the breath fails one.

His connection with the Queen's Hall began in 1895, when he initiated the ever-popular Queen's Hall Promenade Concerts, which are the delight of the bourgeois amateur even unto this day.

In 1897 he started the Queen's Hall Choral Society's Concerts and the Queen's Hall Sunday Orchestral Concerts. The Sunday afternoon concerts are consequently in their ninth season. They are now under the auspices of the Sunday Concert Society, whose president is the Duke of Portland. The Queen's Hall Orchestra, on the other hand, is the affair of a limited company with Sir Edgar Speyer, Bart., for chairman, and Earl Howe and Lt.-Col. Arthur Collins, C.B., among the directors.

Personally, Mr. Wood is what one would term a fine figure of a man with a considerable dark beard. And he allows his hair to grow long – this, of course, being an artistic necessity. In spite of his hirsute adornments, however, he is a fairly obvious Englishman and reminds one more of a farmer who has neglected to go to the barber's than of a heaven-born genius.

Unlike Sousa and Mr. James Glover, Mr. Wood exhibits few, if any, conductorial eccentricities; being, indeed, an austere sort of a bâton-waver who knows his business and does not go in for fireworks. There are critics in the world who believe him to be the only properly inspired conductor now alive. His admirers agree with those critics, and his admirers number tens of thousands of persons who love music sufficiently well to be discriminate about it.

Professionally, too, Mr. Wood is both popular and esteemed. His own orchestra worships him and his fellow-musicians frankly admit that he has great gifts, and that he has probably done more for music in England, and particularly in London, than the rest of our conductors put together. His ability and good sense coupled with exceptional musicianly enthusiasm and a modesty quite unusual in so public a man have endeared him to troops of professional friends. Like Lord Roberts he does not advertise, but sticks solidly to his Wagner, his Tschaikowsky, his orchestra, and his Queen's Hall public, which, on the whole, is about as fine and appreciative a public as a conductor could desire.

Mr. Wood was born in London on March 3rd, 1870. He is understood to have given vocal entertainments in his cradle. At nine years of age he occupied the important post of deputy-organist at St. Mary's, Aldermanbury. So that he may be counted among the erstwhile infant prodigies who have lasted. He is not yet a knight, but he married a princess (Princess Olga Ourousoff of Podolia, Russia), which is the next best thing. He lives at No. 4, Elsworthy Road, N.W., and his telegraphic address, if you please, is 'Conducteth, London.' We wish him long life and plenty of Wagner."

Vanity Fair, 17 April 1907

Mr. Henry Wood

'Tony'

SPY (SIR LESLIE WARD) (1851-1922)
Allan Aynesworth

Allan Aynesworth was the stage name of the stage and screen actor Edward Abbot-Anderson (1864-1959). In 1895, he played the lead role of Algernon Moncrieff in the world premiere of Oscar Wilde's *The Importance of Being Earnest*, performed at the St James's Theatre, London. His final role was alongside Richard Burton in the 1949 film, *The Last Days of Dolwyn*.

'Tony'

"Allan Aynesworth, commonly known to his friends as 'Tony' was born in the year of grace 1865 at the Royal Military College Sandhurst. His father, General E. Abbot-Anderson, was attached for many years to this forcing-house for budding officers, and brought up there not only Allan Aynesworth, but his six brothers, who have, for the most part prospered in life beyond what their neighbours regard as seemly; the eldest, for instance, Colonel Abbot-Anderson, being now in command of the Legation Guard at Pekin; while another brother, Dr. Abbot-Anderson, M.V.O., is Physician in Ordinary to H.R.H. the Princess Royal. Allan Aynesworth was educated in France and Germany, but at length managed, like every true son of Ireland, to get his own way, and show himself before the footlights.

He served his stage apprenticeship (a very useful one) in the late Sarah Thorne's Stock Company. His London début was made under Messrs. Hare and Kendal's management at the St. James's Theatre. Since that eventful day – or rather night – he has never looked back. During the past eighteen years he has played at nearly every West-End theatre. Till lately he was associated in the various productions of the Comedy Theatre, and scored a conspicuous success in that brilliant comedy 'The Truth,' whilst his performances in the 'Freedom of Suzanne,' 'All-of-a Sudden Peggy,' 'Angela,' and 'Lady Barbarity' have all added to his popularity. He is now acting with Mrs. Langtry in 'A Fearful Joy' at the Haymarket. His favourite parts are Charles Surface and George D'Alroy, which he played at the Haymarket Theatre.

He is a member of the Beefsteak and Garrick Clubs. He is a keen sportsman, greatly addicted to grouse shooting, and his happiest days have been spent on the moors. In fact, love for the country and enthusiasm for his work are his two great interests in life.

His pet bugbears are bad food, bad parts, and badly cut clothes. He also owns to a dislike for rehearsals. 'They are improper,' according to him, just as a celebrated mathematician once spoke of a triangle as amiable.

He inhabits a charming flat in the neighbourhood of Langham Place – a flat full of beautiful things, in which Adam decorations, Chippendale and Sheriton furniture, old Sheffield plate, and chintzes play such an important part that it makes one understand that it is possible to have taste without a woman's influence.

He has one great ambition in life – an impossible one – 'to be thought a good actor by everyone of his audience.'"

Vanity Fair, 20 May 1908

85
SPY (SIR LESLIE WARD) (1851-1922)
Allan Aynesworth
'Tony'
Signed
Watercolour and bodycolour
19 x 12 ½ inches
Illustrated: *Vanity Fair*, 20 May 1908, Men of the Day no 1119, 'Tony'

VANITY FAIR Supplement.

"The Canadian Pacific."

SPY (SIR LESLIE WARD) (1851-1922)
Sir Thomas Shaughnessy

Thomas Shaughnessy (1853-1923) was born in Wisconsin, USA, where he began a career on the Milwaukee Railway. In 1882, he was made general manager of the Canadian Pacific Railway and moved to Montreal, where he would remain for the rest of his life. In 1891 he became the company's vice-president, before becoming its president in 1899. For his services to the growth of Canada's industry, he was knighted in 1901 and raised to the peerage in 1916.

'The Canadian Pacific'

"Of that Irish stock which does better everywhere else in the world than it does in Erin, Thomas Shaughnessy was born in Milwaukee, Wisconsin, in 1853: he had the ordinary public school education of the American lad, and at sixteen, by his own desire, he went in for railway work and got a place as clerk in the purchasing department of the Chicago, Milwaukee and Saint Paul Railway. The boy was, of course, filled with ambition; but it is very unlikely indeed that his boyish ambition ever soared higher than the reality.

A very glutton for work, Thomas Shaughnessy in a few years became general storekeeper, and had to look after the distribution of the supplies over the whole system. It was in this way that he came in contact with William Van Horne, who was at that time General Superintendent of the railway. A little later, William Van Horne went to Canada, and in 1882 he sent for Thomas Shaughnessy, and made him the Purchasing Agent, with an office in Montreal, for the Canadian Pacific Railway, which was just about to be started.

Only one man living can tell the history of the Canadian Pacific Railway, and that man is Sir Thomas Shaughnessy. His life history is the history of the great steel girdle. Five men formed themselves into a syndicate and undertook to construct the railway: they were George Stephen, now Lord Mount Stephen, who was the initiating genius of the line, and the first President of the Company. He had been building the Saint Paul, Minneapolis and Manitoba road, with James J. Hill, and made a lot of money; he was the first man to see that the Canadian Pacific Railway was at least as feasible as the Union Pacific. The others were Donald A. Smith, now Lord Strathcona, William Van Horne, R. B. Anzus and Duncan Macintyre. Hill retired very quickly because of a disagreement with his colleagues.

It all looks very easy now; but financing the railway was very difficult. It was thought at first that sixty-five million dollars of common stock, with a Government subvention of twenty-five million dollars would suffice to construct the whole road; but it was almost impossible to sell the shares. Still, the construction of the road went on: two men being determined to see it through, George Stephen and Donald Smith. These two found millions of dollars for the railway as and when they were wanted. But in 1884-5 it was necessary to borrow from the government; thirty million dollars were borrowed on bonds, giving the whole of the completed line, rolling stock, stations and everything as security. Sir John Macdonald, the Premier of Canada, did his best, and carried the loan through: the loan was all repaid before the end of 1885, by an issue of thirty-five million dollars in bonds. As soon as the road was completed these bonds were taken up, and the financial stress was lifted, but of course even then the road was not a paying property; branch lines and feeders had to be constructed; but in measure as this was done the road prospered.

Before this Sir Thomas Shaughnessy had made himself a marked man: in 1885 he was appointed Assistant General Manager under Van Horne: in 1891 Lord Mount Stephen retired and Mr. Van Horne became President and Thomas Shaughnessy became Vice-President. In 1900 Mr. William Van Horne in his turn retired, and Thomas Shaughnessy became President: he was knighted the next year. The Canadian Pacific Railway is regarded by experts as the greatest railway on the American continent: it owns 9,500 miles of road in Canada, will own 10,000 before the end of the year, and controls over three thousand more miles of railway in the United States. It directs a fleet of sixteen steamers between Great Britain, the Continent and Canada. The steamers run to Quebec and Montreal in summer, and to St. John, New Brunswick, in winter: the two Empress vessels are among the finest steamers afloat: the railway also manages a line of steamers from Vancouver to Japan, China and Hong Kong, and possesses three high-class passenger boats. It has also trading steamers running up the Pacific Coast between Vancouver and Alaska, and vessels on all the lakes, especially on Lake Superior.

As Sir Thomas Shaughnessy says, 'The Canadian Pacific has already given the All-Red Route: if the English want it improved, it can be improved at a very small cost: if the British government wishes to give a subvention for the carrying of mails, we will undertake to deliver mails and passengers in Chicago from Great Britain a day sooner than they can be delivered via New York.'

Sir Thomas Shaughnessy is very proud of Canada and of its future. The Goldwin Smiths, he says, and the Judge Longleys have no following: 'Canada is not going to cut loose from the mother country: we do not regard ourselves merely as a colony: but as a sister nation: we wish to have more voice in such affairs as concern us chiefly; but we believe that the connection with the mother country will become even closer with time, and with improvements in the ways of communication.'

Sir Thomas Shaughnessy was married in 1880 and has five children, two boys, and three girls.

When the history of the Canadian Pacific Railway and the development of Canada comes to be written, the two names of Lord Mount Stephen and Sir Thomas Shaughnessy will be found linked together indissolubly: the first was the inaugurating genius, the second brought the great line to assured success and the first place among Transcontinental railways."

Vanity Fair, 26 August 1908

86
SPY (SIR LESLIE WARD) (1851-1922)
Sir Thomas Shaughnessy
'The Canadian Pacific'
Signed
Watercolour and bodycolour
18 x 14 ¾ inches
Illustrated: *Vanity Fair*, 26 August 1908, Men of the Day no 1133, 'The Canadian Pacific'

SPY (SIR LESLIE WARD) (1851-1922)
Frank Shuttleworth (1845-1913)

After being educated variously in England, France and Germany, Frank Shuttleworth (1845-1913) joined the military and served firstly in Ireland before travelling to India as Cornet in the 11th Hussars in 1866. He returned to England in 1869, transferring to the 7th Hussars. He served as captain for 12 years before becoming a major. After retiring from the army in 1882, he became well-known as a sportsman. He owned the successful shooting estates of Old Warden and Goldington in Bedfordshire, and owned a number of winning racehorses, which he even rode to victory several times himself. He also held the position of Director of the Great Northern Railway Company for over 25 years.

'Charlie'

"Colonel Frank Shuttleworth is a warm advocate of that variety of occupations which is the greatest recreation in life. He has somehow contrived to carry on that series of parallel existences which, according to Renan, is the strongest desire of all richly endowed natures. He is a soldier, politician, yachtsman, huntsman, linguist, railway-director, and man-about-town, and is still young enough in spirit to make his mark in half-a-dozen other directions.

He was born in 1845, educated in France and Germany, and in 1866 sailed to Bombay as Cornet in the 11th Hussars. After two seasons Ibex shooting in Cashmere he returned to England in 1869, and exchanged to the 7th Hussars, in which regiment he served for twelve years as captain and then as major.

In 1882 he retired from the Army and took upon himself the dignities of family representation, succeeding on his father's death to the Old Warden and Goldington estates in Bedfordshire. The Old Warden estate is famous for its pheasant and partridge shooting, fifteen hundreds birds being the usual bag with six guns.

He is a good all-round sportsman, has had a good many successes on the Turf, and after winning the 7th Hussars Regimental Challenge Cup two years in succession he lost it the third year by a head, being beaten by a horse he had just sold. He himself rode one of his own horses in fourteen steeplechases, of which he won nine.

Colonel Shuttleworth has been a member of the Royal Yacht Squadron twenty years, and is a prominent member of the Four-in-Hand and the Coaching Club. In spite of numerous invitations, he has steadily declined to go into Parliament, preferring to exercise his business abilities in some less barren field. For twenty-five years he has been a director of the Great Northern Railway Company, where his sound business capacity has long been recognised. He is a valuable Conservative, and under the blessed English system of division, in which one class does all the work and another reaps all the honours, has succeeded in evading a good deal of publicity.

He possesses in a high degree the qualities which make for popularity, and although his character is dignified by reserve, he is simple and unaffected."

Vanity Fair, 10 February 1909

87
SPY (SIR LESLIE WARD) (1851-1922)
Col. Frank Shuttleworth
'Charlie'
Signed
Inscribed with title below mount
Inscribed 'Shuttleworth' on reverse
Watercolour and bodycolour
20 x 14 inches
Illustrated: *Vanity Fair*, 10 February 1909, Men of the Day no 1158, 'Charlie'

'The Greatest Living Frenchman.'

88
Jean Baptise Guth (1883-1921)
Anatole France
'The Greatest Living Frenchman'
Signed, inscribed with title and dated 1909
Pastel on tinted paper
22 x 14 inches
Illustrated: *Vanity Fair*, 11 August 1909, Men of the Day no 1184,
'The Greatest Living Frenchman'

Jean Baptise Guth (1883-1921)
Anatole France

Beginning a literary career as a journalist and poet,
Anatole France (1844-1924) rose to become one of France's most
celebrated novelists and intellectuals. He achieved fame with
novels such as *Le Crime de Sylvestre Bonnard* (1881),
La Rôtisserie de la Reine Pédauque (1893) and *Les Opinions de
Jérôme Coignard* (1893) and was elected to the Académie
Française in 1896. His later works, such as *L'Île des Pingouins*
(1908) and *La Révolte des Anges* (1914), satirised human nature,
political and ideological fanaticism and Catholicism, to the point
where, in 1922, his entire body of work was placed on the
Catholic Church's Index Librorum Prohibitorum (list of banned
books), something that France considered a 'distinction'. He was
awarded the Nobel Prize for Literature in 1921.

'The Greatest Living Frenchman'

*"Jacques Anatole, Thibault took the name of Anatole France and
has made it world-famous, not only by his writings, but also by
noble living. He loves to tell you that he was born in Paris itself,
in 1844 – a child of the streets and quays.' He went to the famous
lycée Stanislaus and even before his baccalauréat became known
to his contemporaries for his exquisite Latin and French prose.
His first book made his literary reputation: his French was at once
acknowledged to be finer than Renan's; as easy and as polished as
the prose of the elder master; even more rhythmic and shot through
with delicious irony – a delight to the spirit. 'Le Crime de Sylvestre
Bonnard,' which appeared in 1881, has been followed by a dozen
masterpieces, all distinguished by the same delicious style, by
originality of outlook, and curiously perfect literary treatment.*

*Now and then, when the story Anatole France has to tell is
dramatic, his erudition plays him sad tricks, gets in his way, and
trips him up like a pair of loose slippers or a sword worn with a
Court suit, which you will. If one had in short space to give a
specimen of Anatole France's genius, one would pick 'Crainquebille,'
which Mr. Bourchier has made familiar to everybody in its English
stage-dress. His works are now being published in English by
Mr. John Lane; some of the translations are excellent, some
indifferent, and others bad; but all readable, thanks to M. France.
Without proofs, however, one may say boldly that Anatole France
is the greatest of living Frenchmen – the greatest writer in
Christendom to-day.*

*He is also very high-minded and honourable. It is a custom in
France that if you wish to be elected to the Academy you must call
on each of the Academicians and ask him for his vote. Anatole
France thought this a custom to be honoured in the breach; he
refused to solicit any man's vote, and the Academicians were
wise enough to bow to his honourable scruple and elect him in
spite of his recalcitrance. A little later the Academicians elected a
certain personage on account of his rank, and not because of his
merit as a writer. M. Anatole France was alone in voting against
his admission, and has since refused to attend any sittings of
the Academy.*

*M. Anatole France is a Socialist and though a sceptic, a believer in
the spirit of the French Revolution of 1780."*

Vanity Fair, 11 August 1909

PIP (ACTIVE 1910)
R E Belilios

Known as 'Billy', Raphael Emanuel Belilios was a barrister and son of a Hong Kong-based businessman and opium dealer. Admitted to the Middle Temple in 1900 and called to the bar in 1903, Belilios occupied chambers at Middle Temple from 1904 to 1922.

'Billy'

"Mr R. E. Belilios, the only son of the late Honourable Emmanuel Raphael Belilios, brings to politics many advantages of temperament and training. He has had much experience at the Bar, to which he was called in 1903, thereafter practising at the North London Sessions. The practice in public speaking and the readiness which such a training brings is supplemented by a degree of self-assurance and decision of potent influence with an average audience. With a varied and complete mental outfit, arranged with legal precision and orderliness, Mr. Belilios gives the impression of being untroubled with doubts and uncertainties. He knows his subjects as a good scholar knows a geometrical proposition, logically and absolutely, but with none of the nuances and half-lights which trouble less gifted men. These characteristics all tend to success in a public man, and it is not surprising to find Mr. Belilios rapidly justifying the predictions of his friends.

Personally, he is one of the most charming of men, with an unassuming manner which it would be unwise to interpret as representing his ultimate opinion of himself. He is a pointed and ready speaker, going instantly to the heart of a matter, and able to express himself with precision and pungency. Few men are better fitted to deal with a hostile audience; his generous frankness, his amusing readiness, and the firmness with which he at all times retains control of affairs wins the respect of his listeners, and his enthusiasm and self-reliance prove contagious. In politics, Mr. Belilios is a strong Tariff Reformer, and is particularly interested in promoting such a union between England and her Colonies as would constitute a really independent Empire. His ideal is, in fact, to develop world commerce so as to constitute a kind of international co-operative society.

Mr. Belilios spends a good deal of his time abroad, at Hong Kong, where he has extensive interests, and has made various lengthy tours in different parts of the world. He is still under thirty, and has all the ability and opportunity necessary to carry him far if he wishes. Everyone speaks well of him, save those who have had the black misfortune to be cross-examined by him. As a cross-examiner he is coldly merciless, and does not indulge in mistaken sympathy for his victim.

Possessed of strong political ambitions, he has every requisite trait to ensure their fulfilment. Unfortunately, he is rich."

Vanity Fair, 6 January 1910

89
PIP (ACTIVE 1910)
R E Belilios
'Billy'
Signed
Inscribed with title and dated '6.i.1910' on reverse
Watercolour
12 x 6 ¾ inches
Provenance: Frank Harris; Stanley Jackson; The John Franks Collection
Illustrated: *Vanity Fair*, 6 January 1910, Men of the Day no 1210, 'Billy'

ELF (SIR LUKE FILDES) (1843-1927)
Archer Baker

Yorkshire-born Archer Baker (1845-1910) emigrated as a young man to Ontario, Canada, to work for the Canadian Pacific Railway. In 1905, he was appointed the European Manager of the CPR. He died of pneumonia in January 1910, the month of his appearance in *Vanity Fair*.

'CPR in Europe'

"Situated opposite the Nelson Monument [the European office] forms one of the landmarks of Trafalgar Square, and Archer Baker, to whose shrewd brain the magnitude of Canadian Pacific interests in Europe is so largely due, may well be proud of this, the tangible proof of his success. Yet no man is more modest"

Vanity Fair, 13 January 1910

Though Archer Baker did appear in *Vanity Fair* on 13 January 1910 as 'Men of the Day no 1212', in later reproductions and albums of *Vanity Fair*, his portrait has been replaced by that of Solomon Barnato Joel (1865-1931), a wealthy businessman and racehorse breeder, painted by an artist who signed 'H.C.O.', about whom little is known. It is possible that this change was made due to Archer Baker's death at the time of his *Vanity Fair* portrait.

90
ELF (SIR LUKE FILDES) (1843-1927)
Archer Baker
'CPR in Europe'
Signed
Inscribed with title and publication details on reverse
Watercolour and bodycolour
17 x 11 inches
Provenance: Frank Harris; The John Franks Collection
Illustrated: *Vanity Fair*, 13 January 1910, Men of the Day no 1212, 'CPR in Europe'
Exhibited: 'Vanity Fair 1869-1914', Church Farm House Museum, Hendon, September-December 1983

VANITY FAIR Supplement

'Through every passion ranging.'

(C. H. Workman)

ELF (SIR LUKE FILDES) (1843-1927)
C Herbert Workman

Charles Herbert Workman (1873-1923) was an actor and singer who rose to fame as part of the D'Oyly Carte Opera Company, which he joined in 1894. By 1897 he was the company's leading comedian, starring in roles in Gilbert and Sullivan productions of *The Mikado*, *The Yeoman of the Guard*, *HMS Pinafore* and many others.

'Through Every Passion Raging'

"Even in his earliest days Mr. Workman was hypnotised by the stage, one of his favourite amusements as a youngster being the production of home-made versions of plays he had seen. These early tastes were looked on with disapproval by his parents, whose pointed protests, however, had little effect. At college the same tastes were in evidence, and at last, in despair, his father, thinking that a dose of the real thing would cure him more effectually than any counsel, agreed to his actually going on the stage. One stipulation, however, was made; he must join one of the D'Oyly Carte companies or none at all. But the stipulation – baffling though it seemed – proved no obstacle, and a little later Mr. Workman joined that company at Bath in 'Utopia, Limited.'

He was called on to take the part of Captain Corcoran at such short notice that the costume for the part – made for a man fully twice his size – could only be adjusted to his modest proportions by numerous tucks. The rest of the cast had not been advised of the change, and when Mr. Workman made his debut, his sword trailing dolefully across the floor, and he himself looking like a child dressed in his father's clothes, the apparition paralysed the whole cast into sudden silence, followed by uncontrollable merriment.

He has played all sorts of rôles in all parts of the earth, but his reputation is, of course, built round Savoy opera and his favourite rôle of Jack Point. He has played that part and the other familiar one of 'Koko' more often than he cares to say, but is still as unwearied as his audiences. The only part of him which gets tired is his tongue, and occasionally the oft-repeated lines have got muddled. 'Self-constricted ruddles,' 'his striggles were terruffic,' and 'deloberately rib me' are a few of the Spoonerisms he has perpetrated, and there are certain lines in his rapidly-sung songs which he always approaches with apprehension. It is the only thing which mars his appreciation of Gilbert and Sullivan opera; an appreciation as keen now as ever.

Success has not spoilt him: he is modest and kindly, in spite of the efforts of hordes of friends to spoil him. He is a perfect storehouse of humorous reminiscence, and is eagerly welcomed 'in places where they sing.'

He is a professional humorist, who has been known to make an Englishman laugh at breakfast."

Vanity Fair, 31 March 1910

91
ELF (SIR LUKE FILDES) (1843-1927)
C Herbert Workman
'Through Every Passion Raging'
Signed
Watercolour and bodycolour
12 x 6 ¾ inches
Provenance: Stanley Jackson; The John Franks Collection
Illustrated: *Vanity Fair*, 31 March 1910, Men of the Day no 1223, 'Through Every Passion Raging'

APE JUNIOR (ACTIVE 1911)
Mr Justice Scrutton

Born into a family that had for several generations ran a shipping line between the United Kingdom and the West Indies, Sir Thomas Edward Scrutton (1856-1934) studied at University College, London and Trinity College, Cambridge, before being called to the bar at the Middle Temple in 1882. He became a KC in 1901, and a bencher of his inn in 1908. He had his own practice, first in Essex Court and then at 3 Temple Gardens, whilst also developing a reputation as an author of law textbooks. In 1909 he was sent as special commissioner on the North-Eastern circuit and in April 1910 was appointed a judge of the King's Bench Division, and in the same year was knighted.

Following his appearance in *Vanity Fair*, in October 1916, he was promoted to the Court of Appeal and became a member of the Privy Council.

'Copyright'

"Alert, incisive, the very, personification of dignified solidity, the Hon. Sir T. Edward Scrutton – apart from his exalted position as one of the judges of his Majesty's King's Bench Division – is, in many ways, a remarkable personage.

He is almost appallingly learned in the law and in the tortuosities of its application to commercial life. What he does not know about copyright is not worth knowing, and as to shipping law he is a walking encyclopaedia.

His scholastic career was a record of continuous successes, exemplifying to the full the value of persistency in intelligent painstaking.

The son of Mr. Thomas Scrutton, shipowner, of Buckhurst Hill, Essex, Mr. Justice Scrutton was born on August 28th, 1856, and first went to Mill Hill School. Thence he proceeded to University College, London (of which he eventually became a Fellow), and completed his academic course at Cambridge University.

At Trinity College, Cambridge, he was a Foundation Scholar. He captured the coveted Senior Whewell Scholarship at the University. His educational achievements make a lengthy list. First Class Moral Science Tripos, 1879, and Senior Law Tripos, 1880, are prominent amongst them. Four times he carried off the Yorke Prize. The University of London gave him his M.A. degree and in the competition for this he obtained marks qualifying for the medal. In gaining his B.A. he took First Class Honours in English, and Honours in Classics and Moral Science; and he got the L.L.B. with First Class Honours in Roman Law and Jurisprudence.

Devoting himself thenceforth to the law, he went to the Inns of Court as Barstow Scholar in 1882, and he was a scholar of the Middle Temple. Thence he received his call to the Bar, and ultimately he was elected a Bencher of his Inn.

As a barrister he acquired a large practice in commercial cases, and engaged assiduously at the same time in literary labours in connection with the legal subjects to which he was devoting particular attention. His 'Treatise on the Law of Copyright' is as authoritative as it is monumental, and so much in request was it

that it quickly passed through four editions. This was given first to the world in 1883; and three years thereafter he published his 'Law of Charter Parties and Bills of Lading,' now in its sixth edition. In 1894 this was followed by another erudite work on the Merchant Shipping Act, also in great demand in legal and commercial circles.

Mr. Scrutton was made a K.C. in 1901, and preferred to a judgeship of the King's Bench Division of the High Court in 1910. Meantime he had acted as counsel to important newspapers, and acquired a position almost unique in matters of copyright, reference, and the like.

Married in 1884 to Mary, daughter of Mr. S. C. Burton, J.P., of Great Yarmouth, he resides at Westcombe Park, and there, in the intervals of his strenuous professional life, has entertained lavishly for his circle of friends is large. In 1886 he contested the Limehouse Division of the Tower Hamlets in the Liberal interest, but was not successful in this his one attempt to enter the House of Commons. He belongs still to the Reform Club, and is a familiar figure at the Atheneum.

His amazing profundity is no bar to the perennial flow of good humour which characterises him as a man."

Vanity Fair, 28 June 1911

92
Ape Junior (ACTIVE 1911)
Mr Justice Scrutton
'Copyright'
Signed and inscribed with title
Ink and watercolour with bodycolour
21 ¼ x 15 inches
Illustrated: *Vanity Fair*, 28 June 1911, Men of the Day no 1227, 'Copyright'

VANITY FAIR Supplement.

"H.R.H."

(H.R.H. The Prince of Wales)

NIBS (FREDERICK DRUMMOND NIBLETT)
(1861-1928)
HRH The Prince of Wales

This portrait depicts the young Edward, at the age of 17. The portrait appeared in *Vanity Fair* the day before Edward was invested as Prince of Wales, at a ceremony at Caernarfon Castle in North Wales. He ascended the throne as Edward VIII in January 1936, following the death of his father George V. In December 1936, Edward abdicated the throne in order to marry the American divorcee, Wallis Simpson.

'H.R.H.'

"His Royal Highness was born on June 23rd, 1894, the event being hailed with the utmost satisfaction and delight throughout the Empire. All the promises of early childhood and boyhood have been amply realised. Like his father, our Sailor King, he was trained for the Navy, which fact without doubt affords satisfaction to the nation.

There is every probability that as time goes on he will fill his position with credit to his parents and to the advantage of the Empire over which, in the ordinary course of nature, at some distant day he will be called upon to rule.

He has been called upon early in life to take part in ceremonial functions, but through the wisdom of the King and Queen there is no need to fear the consequence, for it has been decided that, after the important and historic pageant at Carnarvon, where his Investiture as Prince of Wales took place with all the pomp and ceremony of bygone times, he must settle down to a course of serious preparation for the exalted position he will be called upon to occupy.

At Windsor his Royal Highness was invested with the Insignia of the Most Noble Order of the Garter, and acquitted himself well under somewhat trying conditions. It was a stately ceremony, and the King and Queen were proud, as well they might be under the circumstances. But this occasion was surpassed in homely human sentiment when, at the Coronation ceremony in Westminster Abbey, the King impressed an affectionate kiss upon the cheeks of his son instead of a formal salute.

For a short visit to his great-uncle the Prince will go to Germany in September, before which time he may spend some time in Scotland, where the King and Queen are to undertake an extended tour.

All this journeying, however, is not holiday-making, for his studies are insisted upon and prosecuted all the time, so that when his Royal Highness goes to Oxford he will be soundly advanced in knowledge. Another voyage on an English warship will add to his naval education, and then he will enter the Army.

As pointed out a few weeks ago, the King's own view is that the Heir-Apparent should be at all points in touch with the people."

Vanity Fair, 12 July 1911

93
NIBS (FREDERICK DRUMMOND NIBLETT) (1861-1928)
HRH The Prince of Wales
'H.R.H.'
Signed and inscribed with title
Signed and inscribed with artist's address on reverse
Watercolour and bodycolour
18 ½ x 11 inches
Illustrated: *Vanity Fair*, 12 July 1911, Our Celebrities no 1287, 'H.R.H.'

SPY (SIR LESLIE WARD) (1851-1922)
The Hon Thomas H A E Cochrane, DL, JP

Thomas Cochrane (1857-1951) first served as an honorary lieutenant colonel of the 4th Battalion Argyll and Sutherland Highlanders and in the 93rd Highlanders and the Scots Guards before becoming Unionist MP for North Ayrshire from 1892 to 1910. From 1895 to 1901 he was Parliamentary Private Secretary to Colonial Secretary Joseph Chamberlain, then in 1902 served as Under-Secretary of State for the Home Department.

'North Ayrshire'

"*A representative of two of the most distinguished Scottish families is the Hon. Thomas H. A. E. Cochrane. His mother was Lady Gertrude Boyle, daughter of the sixth Earl of Glasgow, while his father was the eleventh Earl of Dundonald. The father's title descended to his brother, Douglas, the present Earl, who is five years his senior.*

He went to Eton for his schooling, and there he met many of those who later became his closest friends in public life.

His interest in military affairs has always been most keen. In addition to serving in South Africa with distinction, he has served in the 93rd Highlanders and Scots Guards. He has also been honoured with the Hon. Lieut.-Colonelcy of the Argyle and Sutherland Highlanders.

In the political world he has always been a staunch Unionist. Elected to Parliament in 1892 for the North Ayrshire Division, he was re-elected in 1896, and served until the January election of 1910, when he went down in the contest over the Budget, being defeated by the small majority of 238. He did not seek re-election in December, 1910. For a considerable time he was Parliamentary Secretary to the Right Hon. Joseph Chamberlain, and became Under-Secretary for the Home Department in 1902. This position he relinquished in 1905.

The Hon. Mr. Cochrane is a J.P., and also D.L. for Renfrewshire. He is at present on an extended tour through the Canadian Dominion, where he is gaining a much-needed rest after many years of arduous and varied service."

Vanity Fair, 2 August 1911

94
SPY (SIR LESLIE WARD) (1851-1922)
The Hon Thomas H A E Cochrane, DL, JP
'North Ayrshire'
Signed
Inscribed with title on reverse
Watercolour and bodycolour
21 x 14 inches
Illustrated: *Vanity Fair*, 2 August 1911, Men of the Day no 2231,
'North Ayrshire'

SPY (SIR LESLIE WARD) (1851-1922)
Lord Stanley of Alderley

Henry Stanley, 3rd Baron Stanley of Alderley (1827,-1903) was a historian specialising in European exploration and expansion of the sixteenth century. He was Vice-President of the Hakluyt Society, which published his editions and translations, including Ferdinand Magellan's *The First Voyage Round the World* (1874).

Fascinated by all things oriental from a young age, Stanley showed an interest in Arabic while at Eton and − as a confident linguist − began to read it at Cambridge. Leaving university after a year, he became précis writer to Lord Palmerston, the foreign secretary, and worked in various positions in the diplomatic service for over a decade. In 1859, he left the service in order to travel in the Near East and Asia, and reached as far as Indonesia. It was also rumoured that he visited Mecca in order to convert to Islam. Continuing to travel through the 1860s, he made a secret Islamic marriage in 1862, to a Spanish woman, Fabia Fernandez Funes. (They underwent further marriage ceremonies at the register office at St George, Hanover Square, in 1869, and at St Alban's Roman Catholic Church, Macclesfield, in 1874. Only after her death in 1905 was it discovered that Fabia was a bigamist, who had already married in 1851, and whose husband did not die until 1870.)

In 1869, Stanley succeeded his father as the 3rd Baron Alderley and took his place in the House of Lords. However, while intending to announce his conversion to Islam, he seems not to have done so and, despite speaking on questions relating to religion and to India, failed to impress his fellow peers.

As a result of his Muslim principles, he closed the public houses on his Cheshire estate, and ensured that churches built or restored on his land, such as that at Llanbadrig, Anglesey, used exclusively geometrical glass. He was also buried according to Muslim rites.

His nephew, Bertrand Russell, described him as 'definitely stupid', but Muriel E Chamberlain, writing in the *Oxford Dictionary of National Biography*, has countered that he was 'brilliant, eccentric, and unstable' (Matthew and Harrison 2004, vol 52, page 214).

95
Spy (Sir Leslie Ward) (1851-1922)
Lord Stanley of Alderley
Signed
Inscribed with title and dated 'Oct 1st 1883' below mount
Watercolour with bodycolour
10 ½ x 7 ¼ inches
Illustrated: Drawn for but not illustrated in *Vanity Fair*

96
LIB (LIBORIO PROSPERI) (1854-1928)
Beast of Burden
Signed and dated 84
Watercolour, bodycolour and pastel on tinted paper
17 ½ x 13 ½ inches
Illustrated: Possibly drawn for but not illustrated in *Vanity Fair*, 1884

97 (opposite)
LIB (LIBORIO PROSPERI) (1854-1928)
Lord Randolph Churchill
Signed and dated 1893
Watercolour on tinted paper
12 ¾ x 8 ¼ inches
Illustrated: Drawn for but not illustrated in *Vanity Fair*, 1893

Lord Randolph Churchill

The father of wartime Prime Minister Winston Churchill, Lord Randolph Churchill (1849-1895) first rose to prominence in the House of Commons as a member of what became known as the 'Fourth Party', a group of young Conservatives extremely critical of not only the Liberal opposition but also the Conservative front bench. In 1880, Churchill appeared in a caricature by Spy in *Vanity Fair* as part of this group, along with Sir Henry Drummond-Wolff, Sir John Gorst and Arthur Balfour. Churchill's first cabinet position was Secretary of State for India from 1885 to 1886 under Lord Salisbury. On 3 August 1886 he was appointed Chancellor of the Exchequer and Leader of the House of Commons. He held these positions until December of the same year, when he suddenly resigned.

98

SPY (SIR LESLIE WARD) (1851-1922)
An Elegant Gentleman
Signed and dated 1907
Watercolour and bodycolour on tinted paper
18 x 12 inches

Dated 1907 but unpublished, the sitter is currently unidentified. That the portrait is signed 'Leslie Ward' and not 'Spy' suggests that this may have been a commissioned portrait and not produced for publication in *Vanity Fair*.

99

ASTN (ALAN HENRY STERN) (1884-1974)

Gentleman with Hands in his Pockets

Signed and dated 13

Extensively but indecipherably inscribed on reverse

Watercolour and bodycolour on tinted paper

14 x 7 ¾ inches

Illustrated: Drawn for but not illustrated in *Vanity Fair*

Spy (Sir Leslie Ward) (1851-1922)
George Grossmith Jr

George Grossmith Jr (1874-1935) was an actor, director, playwright and producer, particularly of Edwardian musical comedies. He was the son of George Grossmith (1847-1912), the writer and composer of comic operas and musical sketches who most famously created a series of characters in the operas of Gilbert and Sullivan and wrote, in collaboration with his brother Weedon, the 1892 comic novel *The Diary of a Nobody*. George Grossmith himself appeared in *Vanity Fair* on 21 January 1888 as 'Men of the Day no 393, "The Pinafore"'.

George Grossmith Jr began his acting career in musical stage comedies such as *Gaiety Girl* (1893) and *The Shop Girl* (1894). He found fame in the early years of the 1900s thanks to a number of musical productions that he often wrote and starred in himself, such as *The Spring Chicken* (1905), *The New Aladdin* (1906) and *Peggy* (1911). Tall and lanky, George Grossmith Jr was often paired with the diminutive actor Edmund Payne for comedic effect. Later in his career, he found success as a producer both in London and New York, with productions such as *The Bing Boys Are Here* (1916), *Kissing Time* (1919) and *Eastward Ho!* (1919).

100
Spy (Sir Leslie Ward) (1851-1922)
George Grossmith Jr
Signed
Watercolour and bodycolour
19 ¾ x 13 inches
Illustrated: Drawn for but not illustrated in *Vanity Fair*

101
SPY (SIR LESLIE WARD) (1851-1922)
Sir Benjamin Leonard Cherry
Signed
Watercolour and bodycolour
18 x 10 ½ inches
Illustrated: Drawn for but not illustrated
in *Vanity Fair*

Sir Benjamin Leonard Cherry (1869-1932) was
a lawyer who was called to the bar at Lincoln's Inn in
1893 and practised as a conveyancer and draftsman
of parliamentary bills. An authority on land law, he
was author and editor on a large number of works on
the subject. Cherry was also a significant parliamentary
draftsman, and was the main author of the Birkenhead
property legislation. Cherry was knighted in 1922
and made a bencher of Lincoln's Inn in 1927.

102

LIB (LIBORIO PROSPERI) (1854-1928)
Walter L Gladstone of Court Hey

Watercolour with bodycolour

20 x 14 inches

Provenance: The Late R R Lockett, until 1907

Illustrated: Drawn for but not illustrated in *Vanity Fair*

Walter Longueville Gladstone (1846-1919) was the son of Robertson Gladstone, a prominent merchant and Mayor of Liverpool from 1843-1844, and a nephew of William Gladstone, the former Prime Minister.

103
SPY (SIR LESLIE WARD) (1851-1922)
Mr Arthur ...
Signed
Indistinctly inscribed with sitter's name below mount
Watercolour and bodycolour
20 x 9 ½ inches
Illustrated: Drawn for but not illustrated in *Vanity Fair*

Clearly drawn for *Vanity Fair* in Leslie Ward's distinctive style, this undated portrait is inscribed in very faded writing with the sitter's name beneath the mount. Only 'Mr Arthur' can be clearly read, with the surname unclear. As a result, the identity of the sitter has not yet been confirmed.

104
SPY (SIR LESLIE WARD) (1851-1922)
The Reporter
Signed
Watercolour and bodycolour with pencil on tinted paper
12 ½ x 8 ½ inches
Illustrated: Drawn for but not illustrated in *Vanity Fair*

The sitter of this undated portrait has thus far not been identified.

105
CLOISTER (SIR CHARLES GARDEN DUFF) (1852-1914)
The Prince of Wales at the Moulin Rouge
Signed with initials and dated 1899
Watercolour and bodycolour on tinted paper
7 x 10 inches
Provenance: The John Franks Collection
This illustration was not published in *Vanity Fair*.

In 1901, Edward, Prince of Wales, ascended the throne to become
King Edward VII. As prince, Edward had developed a reputation
as a sportsman and carouser. In 1890, a year after the opening of
the famous Parisian cabaret Moulin Rouge, Edward was spotted in
the audience by the popular dancer La Goulue, who reportedly
cried for the prince to buy champagne for everyone.

106 (opposite)
CLOISTER (SIR CHARLES GARDEN DUFF) (1852-1914)
Henry Lucy at Boodles
Signed with initials, inscribed 'Harry' and dated 1899
Watercolour and bodycolour on tinted paper
9 ½ x 8 ½ inches
Provenance: The John Franks Collection

Sir Henry Lucy (1843-1924) was one of the leading journalists of
his day, particularly famous as the writer of *Punch*'s 'Essence of
Parliament' from 1881 to 1916 under the pseudonym 'Toby MP'.
He was briefly a sub-editor of the *Pall Mall Gazette* in early 1870,
before becoming a regular contributor to London's *Daily News*
from 1872. He became the paper's editor briefly in 1885 and in
1897 refused the editorship of *Punch* out of loyalty to Francis
Cowley Burnand, the editor at the time. Lucy's writing for *Punch*
was compiled into numerous volumes: *A Diary of Two Parliaments*
(2 vols, 1885-6); *A Diary of the Salisbury Parliament, 1886-1892*
(1892); *A Diary of the Home Rule Parliament, 1892-1895* (1896);
A Diary of the Unionist Parliament, 1895-1900 (1901); and *The
Balfourian Parliament, 1900-1905* (1906).

In his autobiography *Forty Years of Spy*, Leslie Ward makes
reference to meeting the Reverend R J Campbell (whose portrait
by Spy appeared in *Vanity Fair* on 24 November 1904) at 'one of
Sir Henry Lucy's delightful luncheon parties' (*Forty Years of Spy*,
page 229).

Spy
Sir Leslie Ward, RP (1851-1922),

For almost 40 years, Sir Leslie Ward defined the look of the society paper, *Vanity Fair*. His well observed, meticulously conceived cartoons permanently altered the art of caricature in England. From the cruel and often grotesque caricatures made popular by the likes of Gillray and Daumier, Leslie Ward made caricature acceptable and, indeed, necessary to the who's who of Victorian high society.

Leslie Ward was born at Harewood Square, London (on the site of what is now Marylebone Station), on 21 November 1851. He was exposed to the artistic life from birth as his father, Edward Matthew Ward, and mother, Henrietta Ada Ward, were both professional artists. His father produced historical paintings and his mother was a fashionable painter of portraits. Indeed, the artistic tradition of Ward's family stretched back further still. His maternal grandfather, George Raphael Ward, was a mezzotint engraver and miniature painter, his mother's great-uncle was John Jackson RA, portrait painter in ordinary to William IV, and his great-grandfather, James Ward, was a versatile painter of landscapes, animals and portraits, engraver, lithographer and modeller. His godfather, Charles Robert Leslie, after whom he was named, was also a Royal Academician and father to George Dunlop Leslie, who won the Royal Academy Schools Silver Medal in 1814.

Ward was strongly influenced by the artistic environment in which he found himself as a young child. At the age of four, he holidayed in Calais with his parents, and produced what he considered to be his first caricatures, of a number of French soldiers loitering at the docks. As his parents were popular and highly sociable in artistic circles, the young Ward was introduced to a great number of the Victorian period's most influential literary and artistic figures. The novelist, Wilkie Collins, was a close friend of his parents, as was his brother, Charles Allston Collins, one of the original members of the Pre-Raphaelite Brotherhood. Other artists who visited his parents' studios when he was child included Daniel Maclise, Sir Edwin Landseer, John Everett Millais and William Holman Hunt. Ward was also introduced to the Queen and Prince Consort, who made regular visits to the studio. One such visit was during the progress of one of his father's commissioned pictures, *The Visit of Queen Victoria to the Tomb of Napoleon I*, which was referred to in *The Spectator*'s review of the Royal Academy Summer Exhibition in 1858 as 'a stagey, flashy, vulgar affair, with scarcely a redeeming point'.

Leslie Ward enjoyed a happy childhood. While he was still young, the family moved from Harewood Square to Upton Park, Slough, a rural environment that he adored. His artistic surroundings nurtured his desire to become an artist. Despite this, and the fact the he was a regular sitter for his parents, Ward never received a single lesson from either. His father was actually keen to dissuade him from becoming an artist and wished to see him educated in a more traditional manner. Initially, he attended Chase's School, Salt Hill, near Slough. However, he did not stay long as the school was soon broken up due to the ill health of the headmaster. As a result, he was sent to study at Eton at a younger age than was planned. At the request of his father, his aptitude and love for drawing was not encouraged whilst he was at Eton. Nevertheless, he continued to indulge his passion, regularly drawing the school's masters and his fellow pupils, and so becoming Eton's unofficial caricaturist. While he was still young, the family returned to London, moving to Kent Villa, Kensington, a large house with two studios one on top of the other for his parents. On school holidays, he spent much of his time watching his parents work there, as well as at the temporary studio erected on the terrace of the House of Lords, where he watched his father paint frescoes for the Houses of Parliament.

At the age of 16, Ward turned his attention to modelling and started a bust of his younger brother, Wriothesley Russell Ward. Working on it in his holidays, he finished it in time to submit it to the Royal Academy, where it was accepted and exhibited at the Summer Exhibition of 1867. However, he chose not to follow up on this success, deeming the process too much of a physical and mental strain on him. As a young man, he also indulged in a growing interest in the stage. During his school holidays, he would assist at various playhouses across London by painting scenery and playing in small roles. He first appeared in front of a large audience at the Bijou Theatre in Bayswater as part of an amateur company called 'The Shooting Stars', comprised largely of Cambridge undergraduates.

After leaving school at the age of 16, Leslie Ward travelled to Paris with a group of friends, for little more reason than to enjoy himself and soak up the city's artistic atmosphere. However, his father's desire to see him installed in a secure vocation resulted in Ward entering the office of Sydney Smirke RA, to study architecture. Smirke was a highly respected architect, whose most well-known works include the Carlton Club and the Reading Room at the British Museum. However, the mechanical process of the profession did not appeal to Ward, and his period with Smirke only served to strengthen his resolve to become an artist. After a year, Smirke had completed his work on the exhibition galleries at the Royal Academy's Burlington House and decided to retire. During this time, Ward had been made a member of the Architecture Association, and his father arranged for him to continue his architectural studies with Edward Barry RA. However, when he was informed that his period of study with Barry would last for another five years, Ward declined the offer and resolved finally to tell his father that he wished to pursue a career as an artist. He found an ally in the painter and Royal Academician, William Powell Frith, a close family friend who agreed to mediate between Leslie Ward and his father. The intervention of Frith at last saw his father relent and give his blessing to his chosen career.

His first commission was to end in unfortunate circumstances. Through his father, Ward obtained work undertaking a series of interior drawings for a family friend, a Mrs Butler Johnson Munro. However, after three months' work, Mrs Butler Johnson Munro suddenly died, leaving Ward with just a five pound note he had been paid after his first day. He did not have the heart to send a claim for full payment to her executors.

A six-week visit to Lord Lytton at Knebworth, in the company of his parents, gave Ward his first real encouragement that he could succeed as an artist. During his stay, he painted a watercolour of Knebworth's great hall and had Lord Lytton sit for a portrait. (He also caricatured his host from memory.) On his return home, his painting of the great hall was accepted by the Royal Academy and, determined to win his father's approval, he began his preparation to enter the Royal Academy Schools. This preliminary course of instruction included study at the Slade School of Fine Art, under Professor Edward Poynter. In 1871, following an extended holiday with friends in Scotland, he entered the Royal Academy Schools as probationer in Architecture, before becoming a full-time student.

Much of his time at the Royal Academy of Arts was spent exhibiting portraits in oil and watercolour and he could easily have made a career in that field. Portraits that he exhibited at the Royal Academy included drawings of his brother, Wriothesley, and his sister, Beatrice. Though he exhibited great talent in portrait painting, and would be elected to the Royal Society of Portrait Painters in 1891, he still held a great love for caricature and continued to draw the various personalities who crossed his path.

Leslie Ward's association with the society paper, *Vanity Fair*, began with a garden party hosted by Lord Leven. Here, he observed the eminent zoologist, Professor Richard Owen, who was nicknamed 'Old Bones'. So taken by what he described as his 'antediluvian incongruity', he resolved to caricature him. At this time, Thomas Gibson Bowles, the founder of *Vanity Fair*, had grown dissatisfied with the artists working for him, the absence of his main caricaturist, Carlo Pellegrini, and was searching for new cartoonists. John Everett Millais, having known of Leslie Ward's skill and enjoyment in creating caricatures and his admiration for *Vanity Fair*, called to see a collection of his work. Particularly taken with the caricature of 'Old Bones', he urged Ward to submit it to *Vanity Fair*. He did so, and it was accepted and published in 1873. The cartoon was unsigned, as Bowles did not approve of Ward's original idea for a signature. When Bowles handed Ward a dictionary and suggested he search for a pseudonym, the page fell open on the 'S's' and his eye was caught by 'Spy'.

Following the publication of his first cartoon, Leslie Ward became a permanent staff member at *Vanity Fair* and he was able to turn his attention 'whole-heartedly and with infinite pleasure' to caricature. When he and *Vanity Fair*'s other great cartoonist, Carlo Pellegrini, were first introduced at a social event, Pellegrini jokingly told onlookers that he had taught Ward everything he knew. He laughed it off, knowing it not to be the case, but when numerous journalists believed it to be true and put it into print, Ward grew to regret not correcting the comment. Nevertheless, this first meeting began a lasting friendship and great mutual admiration.

'Spy' was an apt pseudonym for Ward, as he often found himself 'stalking' his subjects everywhere from the law courts and Houses of Parliament to society gatherings and theatres of London, before drawing them from memory. In his early days at *Vanity Fair*, he was often given subjects that were refused by Pellegrini, and his caricatures were often the result of hours of continual attempts, watching his subjects as they walked or drove past. In Thomas Gibson Bowles, Ward found a valuable ally when studying his subjects. As Ward explains, 'he was so thoroughly a man of the world and withal so tactful and resourceful that I was glad when we worked in company. It was a great help for me, and I was able to employ my attention in observing while he took the responsibility of conversations and entertainment of the subject entirely off my hands'. In January 1873, Ward received a commission from William Luson Thomas, editor of *The Graphic*, and contributed a number of portrait drawings to the paper, including those of Sir John Cockburn, Benjamin Disraeli, William Gladstone and Lord Leighton. In 1876, he left *The Graphic* and worked exclusively for *Vanity Fair* alongside Pellegrini. When Pellegrini died in 1889, Ward produced virtually every cartoon.

In 1874, his parents had left London and moved to Windsor. As Ward was required to stay in London, he took rooms in Connaught Street, and a studio in William Street, Lowndes Square. As his fame grew and his time became more precious, he began to require many of his subjects to come to this studio and sit for him.

This procedure frequently irritated him, as his sitters often made requests as to how they should be portrayed, or complained about the final result. Nevertheless, he continued to accept commissions to produce portraits, partly because he remained greatly fond of the process of portrait painting, but also because it was well paid. In an 1897 interview given by Oliver Armstrong Fry, then editor of *Vanity Fair*, to Frank Banfield of *Cassell's Magazine*, it was reported that Ward received between £300 and £400 for a portrait. Later in life, he would regret not allowing himself more time to work in this medium.

The nature of his work and his association with such a reputable society magazine as *Vanity Fair* meant that Leslie Ward figured prominently in the upper echelons of Victorian society. In 1874, he joined the Arts Club in Hanover Square, whose members at the time included *Punch* cartoonists John Tenniel and Charles Keene. He later became a member of the Orleans Club, the Lotus Club and the Pelican Club. In 1876, he became one of the original members of the Beefsteak Club, a bohemian club founded by Archibald Stuart Wortley. He was elected an honorary member of the Lyric Club, and also joined the newly opened Fielding Club and the Gallery Club, held on Sunday nights at the Grosvenor Galleries. In July 1880, he was invited on a cruise aboard the HMS Hercules by the Duke of Edinburgh, who had seen and admired his caricature of the Admiral Sir Reginald MacDonald, which had appeared in *Vanity Fair*. In 1890, he was given the honour of a sitting by the Prince of Wales at Marlborough House.

After many years as a bachelor, Leslie Ward married in 1899 to society hostess Judith Topham-Watney, the only daughter of Major Richard Topham, of the 4th Queen's Own Hussars. They had initially courted some years earlier, only for her parents to block their engagement on the grounds that Ward was financially unworthy. However, in 1899 they happened to meet again on a train journey, their relationship was rekindled and they were married a few months later at St Michael's Church in Chester Square. Settling down together in Elizabeth Street, Belgravia, they had one daughter, Sidney.

In 1911, Leslie Ward resigned from *Vanity Fair*, ending an association with the paper that had lasted almost 40 years. He was soon approached by the paper, *The World*, who offered him not only the same pay that he received at *Vanity Fair*, but also permission to retain the rights of his original drawings. As a result, he was able to send a collection of his works to the Turin Exhibition at the request of Sir Isidore Spielmann, for which he received a Grand Prix. He also occasionally produced portraits for *Mayfair*, which Ward described as 'the only Society journal that I can recall having succeeded in any way on the lines of *Vanity Fair*' [*Forty Years of 'Spy'*, page 337]. In 1914, he was commissioned by the staff of the *Pall Mall Gazette* and *The Observer* to produce a portrait of their editor, James Louis Garvin.

In 1915, Leslie Ward published his autobiography, *Forty Years of 'Spy'*. He was knighted in 1918. He died suddenly of heart failure at 4 Dorset Square, London, on 15 May 1922.

His work is represented in the collections of the National Portrait Gallery.

Further reading:
Peter Mellini, 'Ward, Sir Leslie [*pseud.* Spy] (1851-1922)', H C G Matthew and Brian Harrison (eds), *Oxford Dictionary of National Biography*, Oxford University Press, 2004, vol 57, pages 325-326; Leslie Ward, *Forty Years of 'Spy'*, London: Chatto & Windus, 1915

Ape
CARLO PELLEGRINI (1839-1889)

Alongside his colleague Leslie Ward (who took the pen name 'Spy'), Carlo Pellegrini defined the look of the Victorian society journal, *Vanity Fair*. Inspired by the work of Melchiorre Delifco and Honoré Daumier, his caricatures, produced under the pen name 'Ape', had an enduring effect on Victorian high society as a whole. So did Pellegrini himself, as the eccentric Neapolitan caricaturist became known as one of London society's most well-known and well-loved figures.

Carlo Pellegrini was born in Capua, Campania, Italy, on 25 March 1839, a descendent of the Sedili Capuani, an aristocratic landowning family. He was educated at the Collegio Barnabiti, then at the Sant' Antonio in Maddaloni, near Caserta. By the age of 20, he had already established himself as a highly popular figure in Neapolitan high society. He was eccentric and funny, kind-hearted and generous. He quickly earned himself many friends and patrons and delighted many of them by drawing caricatures for them, though he had no formal artistic training.

In the autumn of 1860, it is possible that the young Pellegrini joined the forces of Giuseppe Garibaldi and fought in the last battles against the Bourbons at the Volturno and at Capua. Although this assertion is the subject of debate, as are many of his anecdotes, according to his *Vanity Fair* colleague, Leslie Ward.

On 9 November 1892, Pellegrini met the Prince of Wales during a visit to Naples, and celebrated his coming-of-age with him. This encounter was significant to his future career, as two years later, when he arrived in London, he was quickly ensconced as a close friend and jester in the Prince's social circle. Why he left Italy is unclear, though he maintained to friends that it was a combination of unrequited love and the death of his sister. He claims that he initially endured poverty when he first arrived in London, including periods sleeping rough in Whitehall and Piccadilly, but his reputation and popularity in London's bohemian society rapidly grew.

As he had done in Naples, Pellegrini regularly drew caricatures for his friends and royal companions. These caricatures came to the attention of Thomas Gibson Bowles, who had recently founded the society paper, *Vanity Fair*. He commissioned Pellegrini to produce colour portraits of Benjamin Disraeli and William Gladstone. These portraits were reproduced by Vincent Brooks, then London's premier lithographer and appeared in *Vanity Fair* in January and February 1869 under the pseudonym 'Singe', the French for 'ape'. His drawings were an immediate success and he became a permanent member of staff at *Vanity Fair*, producing caricatures under his new pseudonym, 'Ape'.

In the 1870s, he met and struck up a friendship with Edgar Degas, and the two men produced portraits of one another, Pellegrini's inscribed 'a vous', and Degas' 'a lui'. Remaining as highly sociable in London as he had been in Naples, Pellegrini was a member of the Arts Club from 1874 to 1888, and a member of the Beefsteak Club, along with Leslie Ward. It was here that he first met James McNeill Whistler, who became a great influence on his work. Pellegrini had long aspired to become a portrait painter to the level of Whistler, and twice left *Vanity Fair*, first in 1871 and again in 1876, in an attempt to succeed in this field. However, his talents for caricature did not extend to portraiture and, after his work in this field was poorly received by critics, he returned to *Vanity Fair* early in 1877. Though he was debilitated in his final years by tuberculosis, he continued to produce cartoons for *Vanity Fair* until his death on 22 January 1889.

At barely five feet two inches tall, with a large head and very small feet, Carlo Pellegrini certainly made a huge impression on those he met. He flaunted his homosexuality, at a time when it was dangerous to do so and dressed eccentrically, though flawlessly. As Leslie Ward observed, 'he always wore white spats, and their whiteness was ever immaculate, for he rode everywhere, a fact which probably accounted for his bad health in later years. His boots, too, were the acme of perfection, and his nails were as long and pointed as those of a mandarin' [*Forty Years of Spy*, page 96]. His story-telling at London society gatherings was legendary, despite his struggles with the language. Ward recalled that when regaling his listeners with his stories, 'his English, which was ever poor, stumbles and tripped, for although he was rather too quick to recollect slang terms, his grammar remained appalling, but delightfully naive' [*Forty Years of Spy*, page 97]. Such was his popularity that when he was debilitated by tuberculosis, his fashionable friends raised the money for his care in a private hospital, settled all his debts, and provided the luxuries to which he was accustomed until his death. The Fine Art Society sold a proof from a destroyed plate of his much admired caricature of Whistler, with Whistler's signature, to pay for his gravestone in Kensal Green Roman Catholic cemetery, London.

His work is represented in the collections of the National Portrait Gallery; and the Royal Library, Windsor.

Further reading:
Peter Mellini, 'Pellegrini, Carlo [peud. Ape] (1839-1889)', H C G Matthew and Brian Harrison (eds), *Oxford Dictionary of National Biography*, Oxford University Press, 2004, https://doi.org/10.1093/ref:odnb/21806;
Leslie Ward, *Forty Years of 'Spy'*, London: Chatto & Windus, 1915

Lib
LIBORIO PROSPERI (1854-1928)

Born in the Umbrian town of Foligno in 1854, little is known of
the life of the Italian artist Liborio Prosperi outside of his
contributions to *Vanity Fair*. His first artwork appeared in the
Vanity Fair's pages on 30 November 1885, a double page spread
of the 1885 Newmarket races which featured the future King
Edward VII. This would be the first of 54 artworks and portraits
that he would contribute to *Vanity Fair*, the last of which, a
portrait of Pope Pius X, appeared on 10 December 1903. Jockeys
and other sportsmen were particularly popular subjects. His most
famous image however was an oil painting of the Lobby of the
House of Commons (1886), which was reproduced in the *Vanity
Fair* Christmas Supplement 1886. The work features a number of
the most prominent politicians of the day, including William Ewart
Gladstone, Joseph Chamberlain, Charles Stewart Parnell, Lord
Randolph Churchill and Lord Hartington; and hangs in the
National Portrait Gallery.

Cloister
SIR CHARLES GARDEN DUFF ASSHETON-SMITH (1852-1914)

**Born into wealth and privilege, little is known of the life of
Charles Garden Duff, outside of the extensive lands and titles
of his family. Following an early career in the military, Duff
seems to have supplemented his time as an amateur
caricaturist, producing a number of portraits for *Vanity Fair*
at the turn of the century.**

Charles Garden Duff was born on 16 April 1851 at Ryde, on the
Isle of Wight, to Robert George Duff, the Deputy Lieutenant of
Caernarvonshire, and Mary (neé Astley). He was the second eldest
of three brothers and a sister. In 1859, his elder brother, George,
assumed the surname Assheton Smith, when the Vaynol estate
near Bangor in Caernarvonshire, which included Dinorwig quarry,
was bequeathed to him for his lifetime under the will of Matilda,
widow of his great-uncle, Thomas Assheton Smith (1776–1858).

As a young man, Charles Garden Duff joined the military,
achieving the rank of Captain in the Highland Light Infantry. In
1875, he married Maud Frances Vivian, daughter of the 2nd Baron
Vivian of Glynn and Truro. She died in 1893 and the following
year he married Mary Elizabeth Sheridan. This second marriage
ended in divorce and in 1902 he married Sybil Mary Verschoyle,
daughter of Lieutenant Colonel Henry William Verschoyle.

Little is known of Charles Garden Duff's career as an artist.
His first caricature was published in *Vanity Fair* on 2 March 1899,
a portrait of Lord Justice of the Court of Appeal, Roland Vaughan
Williams, signed with his initials. Another six caricatures were
published in *Vanity Fair*, the last of which appeared on 30 April
1903, all signed with the pseudonym 'Cloister'.

In 1904, his older brother died and the following year Charles
Garden Duff's name was legally changed to Charles Gordon
Assheton-Smith by Royal Licence, and he assumed his brother's
land and title. In 1908, he held the office of High Sheriff of
Carnarvonshire and on 1 August 1911 he was created 1st Baronet
Duff, of Vaynol Park, Bangor, co. Caernarvon. He died on 24
September 1914, at the age of 63.

Coïdé
JAMES [JACQUES-JOSEPH] TISSOT (1836-1902)

*'His work can hardly be called caricature; for the sketches were
rather characteristic and undoubtedly brilliant drawings of his
subjects'* (Sir Leslie Ward)

**Though best known as the French painter of English society,
James Tissot also produced insightful caricatures. These
appeared in *Vanity Fair*, under the name 'Coïdé', in the period
from 1869 to 1873, alongside those of 'Ape' and before the
arrival of 'Spy'.**

The second of four sons of a prosperous linen merchant, James
Tissot was born in Nantes, on the River Loire, on 15 October 1836.
He was educated at Jesuit colleges in Brugelette, Belgium; Vannes,
Brittany; and Dôle, Franche-Comté. He considered becoming an
architect and then an artist. Moving to Paris by 1856, he studied
at the École des Beaux-Arts, under Louis Lamothe and Hippolyte
Flandrin. While there, he befriended James McNeill Whistler and
Edgar Degas. Exhibiting at the Paris Salon from 1859 and at the
Royal Academy of Arts, London, from 1864, he soon abandoned
mediaeval subjects in favour of the elegant, polished, often complex,
contemporary scenes for which he is best known. In 1869, he also
began to produce his first caricatures for Thomas Gibson Bowles's
society paper, *Vanity Fair*, signing them 'Coïdé', 'perhaps because
they were a collaboration between Bowles's notions and Tissot's
draughtsmanship, thus "co-idée"'(Richard Thomson, in Anna
Gruetzner Robins and Richard Thomson, *Degas, Sickert and
Toulouse-Lautrec. London and Paris 1870-1910*, London: Tate,
2005, page 20).

Following the outbreak of the Franco-Prussian War in 1870,
Tissot fought in the defence of Paris, but fled to London a year
later. Through the auspices of Bowles, he made many professional
and social connections, and his work gained rapid popularity.
He lived openly with his Irish mistress, Kathleen Newton, in a
house in Grove End Road, St John's Wood. However, this sojourn
came to an end in 1882 when, having contracted tuberculosis, she
committed suicide at the age of 28.

Tissot returned to France, and soon turned to religion, both as a
way of life and a subject for his art. He even made two visits to the
Holy Land, in 1886-87 and 1889, which inspired a large series of
watercolour illustrations of the Bible. These drawings were exhibited
at the Doré Gallery on his return. On 8 August 1902, he died at
the Château de Buillon, Doubs, Franche- Comté, which he had
inherited from his father in 1888.

His work is represented in numerous public collections, including
the National Portrait Gallery and Tate; Musée d'Orsay; and Brooklyn
Museum (New York) and the Minneapolis Institute of Arts.

Further reading:
Willard E Misfeldt, 'Tissot, James [Jacques-Joseph] (*b* Nantes,
15 Oct 1836, *d* Château de Buillon, Doubs, 8 Aug 1902)',
Jane Turner (ed), *The Dictionary of Art*, London: Macmillan, 1996,
vol 31, pages 29-31

Elf
SIR LUKE FILDES (1842-1927)

Sir Luke Fildes is known as one of the leading figures of the Social Realist movement in the late nineteenth-century. His large scale paintings of the miserable poor were shocking to a public used to rustic landscapes and lovers in period costume. An extremely versatile artist, Fildes was also a talented portrait painter, taking royal commissions to paint Edward VII and George V later in his career. As an illustrator, he produced work for Charles Dickens, and later produced caricatures for *Vanity Fair* under the pen-name 'Elf'.

Luke Fildes was born on 18 October 1842 in Liverpool, the fourth of ten children. As a child, he grew up in a religiously divided household, as his father James Fildes, a mariner and shipping agent, was protestant, but the children had been baptised by their mother, Ellen, as Roman Catholics. At the age of 11, Fildes was sent to live with his grandmother, Mary Fildes. She had been something of a political radical in her youth and initially disproved of her grandson's artistic studies, nevertheless she was a financial support to him.

From 1857 to 1860, Fildes attended evening art classes at Chester's Mechanics' Institute, attaining the position of pupil teacher, before studying full-time at Warrington Art School from 1860 to 1863. He moved to London in October 1863, having won a scholarship to study at the Government Art Training School in South Kensington. It was here that he met Hubert von Herkomer and Frank Holl. All three men would become influenced by the work of Frederick Walker, leader of Britain's social realist movement. In 1865, he entered the Royal Academy Schools, where he studied until the following year. In 1866, he started to work for the wood-engraver and publisher William Luson Thomas, and produced illustrations for a variety of books and periodicals, including *The Quiver*, *Once a Week*, the *Cornhill Magazine*, and the *Gentleman's Magazine*. On 4 December 1869, an illustration by Fildes appeared in the first issue of *The Graphic*, entitled 'Homeless and Hungry' and depicting a line of homeless people applying for tickets to stay overnight in a workhouse. The illustration accompanied an article on the Houseless Poor Act and was brought to the attention of Charles Dickens by John Everett Millais. Dickens was so impressed that the following year he commissioned Fildes to illustrate his final, unfinished novel, *The Mystery of Edwin Drood*, establishing his reputation as a leading illustrator. Twelve illustrations had already been completed when Dickens invited Fildes to join him at Gad's Hill, Dickens home, in order to see first hand the inspiration for the book. About to start his journey to visit Dickens, Fildes learned of the author's death. Dickens' family invited Fildes to come and finish the work he and Dickens had started. Fildes's drawing of Dickens's study after his death, *The Empty Chair*, which first appeared in *The Graphic*'s Christmas number for 1870, was exhibited at the Royal Academy in 1871, and the poignant image of the novelist's death was a huge public success.

Luke Fildes was a skilled oil painter and left *The Graphic* in 1870 to focus on this medium. The fashionable subject, of lovers in period costume, were his submissions to the Royal Academy in 1872 and 1873, before he exhibited a large social realist painting, *Applicants for Admission to a Casual Ward*, modelled on his

illustration for *The Graphic*, at the Royal Academy in 1874. That year, he married Fanny Woods, the sister of his friend Henry Woods. Fanny would model for a number of his works, such as in *Betty*, which was exhibited at the Royal Academy in 1875 and *An al Fresco Toilet*, which appeared at the Royal Academy in 1889. She achieved some success as an artist herself, exhibiting at the Dudley Gallery, London, and at the Royal Academy. Among their seven children was the microbiologist Sir Paul Fildes.

Fildes's second social realist painting, *The Widower* was exhibited at the Royal Academy in 1876 and was, like his first, criticised by a public not used to seeing squalor and misery on such a large scale. Fildes was elected associate of the Royal Academy in 1879, the year in which he completed and exhibited his third social realist painting, *Return of a Penitent*. He regularly visited his friend Henry Woods's home in Venice during the 1880s and produced a series of paintings of working-class women. His fourth large social realist painting, *The Village Wedding*, was exhibited at the Royal Academy in 1883 and despite numerous requests for portraits, he continued to paint genre and Venetian subjects during the 1880s, and turned to portraiture in 1887, the year he became a Royal Academician. His final subject painting, *The Doctor*, was inspired by the final illness of his first-born son, Philip, who had died of tuberculosis in 1877. It became his most enduringly popular and most reproduced painting, appearing in doctors' surgeries everywhere. He was a skilful and successful portrait painter, accepting commissions for state portraits of Edward VII in 1902, Queen Alexandra in 1905 and George V in 1912.

In December 1892, Luke Fildes was caricatured in *Vanity Fair* by Spy, but it was not until 30 December 1908 that he contributed to *Vanity Fair* for the first time himself, with a caricature of the stockbroker and racehorse owner, Paul Nelke. Under the pseudonym 'Elf', he produced 18 portraits for *Vanity Fair* between 1908 and 1910.

He was knighted in 1906 and was created a Knight Commander of the Royal Victorian Order in 1918.

Luke Fildes continued to paint portraits until his death on 27 February 1927 at his home on Melbury Road, Kensington. He was buried at Brookwood cemetery, near Woking, Surrey. His wife, Fanny, died a few weeks later on 3 April 1927 and was buried alongside him.

His work is represented in the collections of the Victoria and Albert Museum.

Further reading:
Janet E. Davis, 'Fildes, Sir (Samuel) Luke (1843–1927)', *Oxford Dictionary of National Biography*, Oxford University Press, 2004
L. V. Fildes, *Luke Fildes, R.A., a Victorian painter*, London: Michael Joseph, 1968

Guth

JEAN BAPTISTE GUTH (1855-1922)

From 1889 until 1908, Jean Baptiste Guth's portraits appeared regularly in *Vanity Fair* alongside those of Leslie Ward ('Spy'). A producer of more studied and less satirical portraits than 'Spy' and the other *Vanity Fair* artists, Jean Baptiste Guth was often chosen to paint some of the paper's most important subjects, such as Queen Victoria, Tsar Nicholas II and French Prime Minister Charles de Freycinet.

Jean Baptiste Guth was born on 4 January 1855 in Paris. On 24 August 1875, he was accepted to study painting at the Parisian École des Beaux-Arts, under the tutleage of Jean-Léon Gérôme and Louis Charles Auguste Steinheil. In 1882, possibly on the recommendation of Steinheil, Guth began work for the renowned stained-glass painter Félix Gaudin, assisting him first with a design for the Crucifixion in the church at Bressuire. In 1885 or 1886, he assisted with further stained glass designs for Clermont Cathedral, a church in Compiègne and Sacré-Coeur in Paris.

In 1883, Guth had travelled to London in an attempt to find work as a portrait painter. On 11 March 1883, his first portrait, that of the French novelist Alphonse Daudet, appeared in *Vanity Fair*. The following year, he began to produce portraits for the Parisian newspaper *L'Illustration*, marking the start of an association that would last over 35 years, with his final portrait appearing in the newspaper in 1920. Guth did not produce another portrait for *Vanity Fair* until May 1889, when he was hired by Thomas Gibson Bowles, the *Vanity Fair* founder, to become a regular contributor to replace Carlo Pellegrini ('Ape') who had died in January 1889. His first portrait upon taking over from Ape was of the French civil engineer Alexandre Gustave Eiffel on 11 May 1889. Between 1889 and 1910, Guth produced over 40 portraits for *Vanity Fair*. Working in watercolour and pastel, his works were often closer studies and less satirical portraits of his subjects. As a result, he was often chosen to produce paintings of some of *Vanity Fair*'s most distinguished subjects, including Queen Victoria (for *Vanity Fair's Diamond Jubilee Supplement*, 17 June 1897), Tsar Nicholas II (21 October 1897) and the German Crown Prince Wilhelm (1 June 1905).

In 1918, the Goupil Gallery in London held an exhibition of Jean Baptiste Guth's portraits of British and French generals, admirals and statesmen, titled 'Men who are running the War, and other celebrities of the Entente'. In its review of the exhibition on 9 March 1918 , *The Graphic* said, 'No finer series of war portraits has been seen in London than those of M. Jean Baptiste Guth ... They are drawn in chalk, and have all been taken from life. They are audacious in their conceptualization, unavoidably annexing the defining feature of the subject. One of the best is that of Viscount Grey. The French series, which includes Poincaré, Clemenceau, Pétain and Foch, is very interesting and more novel to the average Englishman.'

Guth died in Paris in 1922.

Nibs

FREDERICK DRUMMOND NIBLETT, RSA (1861-1928)

Though too little known today, Frederick Drummond Niblett produced some of the most striking caricatures of the Edwardian period in a style reminiscent of the posters and illustrations of William Nicholson and James Pryde, who worked together as the 'Beggarstaff Brothers'.

Frederick Drummond Niblett was born in Edinburgh as possibly the youngest of three children of an English father, the commission agent, Francis Burgess Niblett, and his Irish wife, Eliza (née George). His uncle was Vice Admiral H S F Niblett, and he too was intended for the sea. Educated at Fettes College, he then studied architecture, which led him into an artistic career. In the early 1880s, he worked from 17 Drummond Place (1882) and then from Albert Studios, Shandwick Place (1884), designing posters and painting portraits in oil and watercolours of churches. Two of his views of St Giles' Cathedral were exhibited at the Royal Scottish Academy (1882 and 1884).

Niblett is likely to have moved to London in the mid 1880s to establish himself as an illustrator. His first illustrated book – Thomas Hood's *The Dream of Eugene Aram* – was created in response to a dramatisation of the poem that was produced in London, and was issued in 1887 by a London publisher, The Leadenhall Press. Concerning a celebrated murder of the eighteenth century, Eugene Aram was dramatised by W G Wills, and first produced at the Lyceum Theatre in 1873, with Henry Irving in the title role. Irving had already made a party piece of reciting Hood's original poem, and became associated with the part of Aram, though he reprised it only briefly in 1879 and 1880.

Niblett dedicated his book to Irving's close friend, the actor-manager, John Lawrence Toole. Two decades later, in 1905, he would illustrate a 'Henry Irving Souvenir', as well as producing other caricatures of the actor. All this suggests an association between artist and actor or, at least, a strong theatrical interest.

In 1890, Niblett illustrated a second volume, N H Willis's *Dulcima's Doom and other Tales*, issued by the Edinburgh publisher Grant & Son. However, through the following decade, he evolved into a political cartoonist and caricaturist, contributing to a wide range of periodicals, under the pen name 'Nibs'. These included *The Crown* (1906-7), *Sketchy Bits* (1909), *Vanity Fair* (1909-13) and *The Bystander* (1916).

Niblett was living, as a lodger, at 5 Sandland Street, Holborn, in 1891; at Langham Chambers, Portland Place, in 1896; at 84 Charing Cross Road in 1911; at 7 Charles Street, Knightsbridge, in 1907; and, as a boarder, at 94 Earl's Court Road, Kensington, in 1911.

Frederick Drummond Niblett died in Margate, Kent, on 2 May 1928.

Melchiorre Delfico
MELCHIORRE DELFICO (1825-1895)

Born into a prominent aristocratic family, Melchiorre Delfico was a master of the Neapolitan art of caricature and a highly skilled operatic writer and composer. Though he indulged his great passion for music throughout his lifetime, Delfico's reputation for caricature in Italy was unrivalled. He was a considerable formative influence on the great *Vanity Fair* artist Carlo Pellegrini, and after a visit to London, was able to contribute to the English art of caricature himself, through a collaboration with *Vanity Fair*.

Melchiorre De Filippis Delfico was born in Teramo, in the Abruzzo region of Italy in 1825. One of six children, he was the second son of Gregorio and Marina Delfico. Born into an aristocratic family, his was considered to be the first family of Teramo and his early years were in keeping with his wealthy upbringing. He studied music from the age of 7 and in 1839, at the age 14, he was sent to study art at the Public Drawing School of Teramo, under the direction of Pasquale Della Monica. Aged 16, he moved to Naples to complete his studies under the renowned professor and Latin poet Monsignor Antonio Mirabelli.

Though he admits in his autobiography that he had discovered a 'penchant for caricature' at the age of 10, his first love and the focus of much of his attention was music. In 1844, he composed his first work, *The Jailer of 1793*, to a libretto by Domenico Bolognese. It was first performed at the Teatro Nuovo the following year.

Despite his aristocratic background, Melchiorre Delfico initially struggled financially as a student in Naples and from 1842, he worked a part time job at the Interior Ministry, through his uncle, Baron Genovese. In 1847, his father died and Delfico began to sell caricatures to support himself. Nevertheless, Delfico still considered caricature to be a hobby, admitting that his upbringing meant that he never considered it as a legitimate way to earn a living. Following the Sicilian Revolution of 1848, his brothers Filippo and Troiano were exiled due to their role in riots in Teramo, placing further financial burden on Delfico.

Melchiorre Delfico was fortunate that he was living in Naples during a period in which the city sparkled with creativity and bohemian invention. In 1850 he composed and staged *The Husband of One Hour* and followed this in 1853 with the comedy *The Board of Recruiters*. In 1855, Delfico had his first caricature published in the journal *Omnibus*, founded by the journalist and critic Vincenzo Torelli. He would continue to contribute to *Omnibus* for a number of years, along with several other Italian pictorial journals. Delfico's musical reputation continued to grow and in 1856 he was invited to compose a score that would be played at the sacred feast of the patron saint of Teramo. In 1857, he met the composer Giuseppe Verdi, who was a good friend of Delfico's uncle. The two became close, and Delfico would draw and caricature Verdi on many occasions.

By the 1860s, Melchiorre Delfico had become well established as a leading Neapolitan artist and caricaturist. In 1860, he began working for the newspaper *L'Arlecchino*, producing an illustration on the third page of every issue for several years. Between 1862 and 1863 he regularly produced cartoons for the satirical newspapers *Noah's Ark* and *Pulcinella*. At some point in the mid-1860s, Delfico travelled to London. According to one biographer, Amilcare Lauria, whilst there he produced work for *Punch*, but this seems not to have been the case. It was during this trip that he was first introduced to Thomas Gibson Bowles, the founder of *Vanity Fair*. His first caricature, of Julius de Reuter, Baron de Reuter, the founder of Reuter's News Agency, appeared in the pages of *Vanity Fair* on 14 December 1872. Though his collaboration with *Vanity Fair* was brief, with his final portrait published on 1 February 1873, he was a regular contributor during this period, producing 8 portraits.

From the 1870s, his caricature work decreased and he began again to focus on his passion for music. He used his versatile talent to conduct, sing tenor and compose on numerous pieces. He wrote the libretto and score for two comic operas, *The Master Bombardone* in 1870 and *The Return to Paris After the War* in 1872, and two musicals in 1876, *The Fair*, and *The Lighting*. All of these works were staged at the Theatre of the Philharmonic Society. Though his work in caricature decreased during this period it did not cease entirely, and in 1881, he began to contribute caricatures to the humorous weekly publication *Caporal Terribile*.

The final years of Melchiorre Delfico's life were marred by a series of tragedies. In September 1884, both his eldest son John, in his early twenties, and his 8 year old daughter Bianca died of cholera, which was ravaging Naples at the time. Just over 5 years later, in December 1889, his wife Concetta Sposito also died. Delfico was left to care for at least 7 young children (as many as 11 according to some sources). He lived with his young family in the Neapolitan town of Portici, where he died on 22 December 1895.

ASTN
ALAN HENRY STERN (1884-1974)

Under the pen name 'ASTN', Alan Henry Stern produced nine portraits for *Vanity Fair* during its final months of publication. An aspiring artist in his 20s and heavily influenced by the work of Spy, Stern would go on to enjoy a 50 year career as a portraitist, producing work for publications such as *The Graphic*, *Bystander* and *The Times*.

Alan Henry Stern was born on 9 February 1884 in Hove, Sussex. Though he was encouraged as a young man to enter into a business career, he pursued a livelihood as an artist and began portrait painting.

The first of 9 portraits he produced for *Vanity Fair* appeared on 1 October 1913, with the final published portrait appearing on 14 January 1914, one of the final issues of the publication. In a career spanning over 50 years, Stern produced work for a wide range of journals and magazines, including *The Graphic*, *Bystander* and *John O' London's Weekly*. His early work was heavily influenced by the early *Vanity Fair* portraitists such as Spy, but he began to work in a more true to life style and received sittings from members of the Royal family later in his career. He contributed portraits of artists such as Augustus John and Charles Cundall to *The Times*, and in 1965 an exhibition of his portraits was held at Chelsea Art Club. He died on 12 December 1974 at the age of 90.

THÉOBALD CHARTRAN (ACTIVE 1878)

Théobald Chartran was born on 20 July 1849 in Besançon, eastern France. As a child, he attended the Lycée Victor Hugo in Besançon, where he demonstrated an early enthusiasm for caricature by drawing his teachers. At the age of 18, he entered the École des Beaux-Arts in Paris, where he studied under the painter Alexandre Cabanel. He began exhibiting academic paintings at the French Artists Salon from 1872, winning the Grand Prix de Rome there in 1877 for his work, Prise de Rome par les Gaulois, and a second medal at the Salon in 1881. During his time in Paris, he also developed a reputation as a talented decorator and painter of murals, winning a number of commissions to paint government buildings in the city. He painted murals in the Grand Stairs at the Sorbonne, in the Arts Room in the Paris Townhouse and painted frescoes for the choir of the church in Champigny.

On 18 May 1878, a caricature by Théobald Chartran of Pope Leo XIII was published in *Vanity Fair*. This would be the first of 70 portraits he would have published in *Vanity Fair* between 1878 and 1887, using the monogram 'T'. In around 1881, Chartran moved to London, living for a time at 25 Bedford Street, off the Strand, and exhibiting at the Royal Academy and the Grafton Galleries. His subjects for *Vanity Fair* were often French and Italian figures, including Guiseppe Garibaldi, Umberto I of Italy, Napoléon Joseph Charles Paul Bonaparte and Victor Hugo. His reputation as not only a talented caricaturist but also as a more serious portraitist saw Chartran increasingly in demand. In 1891 he travelled to the Vatican to paint the official portrait of Pope Leo XIII.

In 1893, Chartran made the first of what would become annual voyages to the United States to undertake portraiture commissions. In 1899, the industrialist and art collector Henry Clay Frick commissioned Théobald Chartran to paint the scene of the signing of the peace protocol between Spain and the United States at the end of the Spanish-American War, that had taken place the year before. In 1903, Frick gifted the painting to the United States, and it currently hangs in the Treaty Room of the White House. The reputation of Théoblad Chartran in the United States was such that he was commissioned to paint the portraits of Theodore Roosevelt's eldest daughter, Alice, in 1901, the First Lady, Edith Roosevelt, in 1902, and later the same year, the President himself. However, Roosevelt hated the finished portrait, considering it too soft and feminine and hid it in a dark corner of the White House. It was later destroyed by members of his family.

In 1904, Théobald Chartran was elected a member at the Academy in his home town of Besançon and was made Chevalier of the Légion d'honneur shortly before his death on 16 July 1907, at the age of 57 in Neuilly-sur-Seine, Paris.

His work is represented in numerous public collections, including the National Portrait Gallery, London; the Musee d'Orsay, Paris, Fine Arts Museums of San Francisco, the Museum of Fine Arts, Boston, Carnegie Museum, Pittsburg, and Harvard University Art Museum.

ARTHUR H MARKS (ACTIVE 1889)

Arthur H Marks produced just two portraits for *Vanity Fair*, in 1889. The first of these, published on 27 April 1889, was that of 'Ape' (Carlo Pellegrini), one of *Vanity Fair*'s most celebrated and revered caricaturists alongside 'Spy' (Leslie Ward). It is possible therefore that Marks was a pupil of Pellegrini's. Marks's caricature of Ape was the inspiration for the portrait produced by Harry Furniss for his memoirs *My Bohemian Days*, in which he reminisces about Pellegrini and his time as a writer in *Vanity Fair*.

PIP (ACTIVE 1910)

The portrait of Emmanuel Belilios, published on 6 January 1910, was the only contribution to *Vanity Fair* by artist who signed as 'Pip'.

APE JUNIOR (ACTIVE 1911)

The artist 'Ape Junior' produced 15 portraits for *Vanity Fair* between January and June 1911, including images of King George V and Robert Baden-Powell. Little else is known about the artist, other than the likely influence that the *Vanity Fair* portraits by Carlo Pellegrini had on him, given his choice of pseudonym.

Select Bibliography

Bryant 2000
Mark Bryant,
*Dictionary of Twentieth-Century British Cartoonists
and Caricaturists,*
London: Ashgate Publishing, 2000

Bryant and Heneage 1994
Mark Bryant and Simon Heneage,
Dictionary of British Cartoonists and Caricaturists 1730-1980,
Aldershot: Scolar Press, 1994

Cohen 1997
Morris L Cohen,
*The Bench and Bar, Great Legal Caricatures from
'Vanity Fair' by Spy,*
New Haven, CT: Hugh Lauter Levin Associates, 1997

Feaver 1981
William Feaver,
*Masters of Caricature. From Hogarth and Gillray
to Scarfe and Levine,*
London: Weidenfeld and Nicolson, 1981

Fildes 1968
L V Fildes,
Luke Fildes, RA, a Victorian painter,
London: Michael Joseph, 1968

Lynch 1926
Bohun Lynch,
A History of Caricature,
London: Faber and Gwyer, 1926

Matthews and Mellini 1982
Roy T Matthews, Peter Mellini,
In 'Vanity Fair',
Berkeley, CA: University of California Press, 1982

Matthew and Harrison 2004
H C G Matthew and Brian Harrison (eds),
Oxford Dictionary of National Biography,
Oxford University Press, 2004 (61 vols)

Turner 1996
Jane Turner (ed),
The Dictionary of Art,
London: MacMillan, 1996

Ward 1915
Leslie Ward,
Forty Years of Spy,
London: Chatto & Windus, 1915

Alphabetical List of Sitters

Unnamed Sitters